THE COMMUNION OF SAINTS

The Communion of Saints

Prayers of the Famous

Introduced and
edited by

HORTON DAVIES

WILLIAM B. EERDMANS PUBLISHING COMPANY
GRAND RAPIDS, MICHIGAN / CAMBRIDGE, U.K.

Copyright © 1990 by Wm. B. Eerdmans Publishing Co.
255 Jefferson Ave. S.E., Grand Rapids, Michigan 49503 /
P.O. Box 163, Cambridge CB3 9PU U.K.

Paperback edition 1996

Printed in the United States of America

01 00 99 98 97 96   7 6 5 4 3 2

Library of Congress Cataloging-in-Publication Data

The communion of saints: prayers of the famous /
introduced and edited by Horton Davies.
         p.   cm.
       ISBN 0-8028-4303-4
    1. Prayers.   I. Davies, Horton.
       BV245.C625   1990
 242'.8 — dc20   90-35714
                                         CIP

The editor and publisher gratefully acknowledge permission to reprint copyrighted
works granted by the publishers listed on p. 154.

CONTENTS

INTRODUCTION

This introduction answers three questions that may be in the mind of the reader. First, what is the meaning of the title of this book? Second, who are the famous authors of the prayers? Third, what are the major types of prayers included and in what order are they arranged?

I

You may be wondering about the title of the book: *The Communion of Saints: Prayers of the Famous.* "The communion of saints" means the vast family of Christians united in their devotion to Christ. This part of the title refers not only to Christians who are our contemporaries but also to the Christians of the past cheering on the Christians of the present* and encouraging them in the obedience of faith, in the hopeful prospect of eternal life, and in the love which Saint Paul considered the supreme Christian virtue. But "saints," you ask—surely these are the perfectly holy? No, I reply, they are mainly in the process of becoming holy and more

---

* The editor has sometimes changed the *thee, thou, thy* language of the older prayers to the contemporary language of *you* and *your*, which reflects our approach to God today. This changes the antiquated form of certain prayers—those of John Donne, for example—and makes them much more relevant. But no other changes of any significance have been made.

dedicated to God. This is the New Testament meaning of the term "called to be saints," in which intention rather than achievement is stressed.

But, you argue, doesn't the subtitle of this book—*Prayers of the Famous*—contradict my explanation of the main title? Doesn't it imply the great saints? On the contrary, given my definition of "saints"; indeed, very few of those whose devotions are included in this collection are thought of primarily as saints. Their prayers are included to show that important people who enacted large roles—not bit parts—on the stage of their times, and who were not secluded and protected in part like monks and nuns, needed to pray and were helped by prayer. Their prayers are for the encouragement of beginning Christians as well as for the comfort of maturing Christians.

II

The authors of these prayers played many different parts in the public arena and illustrate a variety of callings and professions.

Inevitably, many were men and women of letters, for such are experts in clarity and concision of style, and most of those chosen were poets with a gift for creating memorable metaphors and vivid images. There are, in fact, twenty poets in this anthology, and one of them, John Donne (Dean of St. Paul's Cathedral, London), contributed thirteen prayers. Others of his age also represented are George Herbert, who preferred the quiet vicarage of Bemerton to being public orator of Cambridge University; John Milton; John Dryden; Anne Bradstreet of New England; Thomas Traherne; Henry Vaughan; and the worldly parson Robert Herrick. Robert Burns, Charles Wesley, William Cowper, and William Blake reflect the succeeding age of sensibility. The nineteenth-century prayers selected were crafted by such poets as Tennyson and Browning, Whittier and Longfellow, Gerard Manley Hopkins and Christina Rossetti.

Eight novelists are also among the company: Robert Louis

Stevenson, Charles Kingsley, George MacDonald, Winifred Holtby, Henry Van Dyke, G. K. Chesterton, C. S. Lewis, and Alan Paton. Other distinguished litterateurs include the dramatists Thomas Dekker and George Bernard Shaw, the essayists Sir Thomas Browne, Joseph Addison, Samuel Johnson, and Theodore Parker, and the diarist John Evelyn.

Philosophers, artists, musicians, and scientists are in short supply in this anthology; but those included here, who wrote admirable prayers, were at the very top of their professions. They include Pascal and Kierkegaard, Dürer and Michelangelo, Beethoven and James Clerk Maxwell.

Eleven statesmen are represented by their orisons: Four were presidents of the United States: Washington, Lincoln, Wilson, and Franklin Delano Roosevelt. Two were British prime ministers: Gladstone and Lord Salisbury; two were lord chancellors of England: Sir Thomas More and Francis Bacon (Baron Verulam). Other men of distinction in politics included are King Alfred, King Charles I, and Dag Hammarskjöld, former secretary-general of the UN. Also included are three philanthropists who had a political impact: Anthony Ashley Cooper (Earl of Shaftesbury), who worked in Parliament to improve the working conditions of women and children in factories; William Wilberforce, the parliamentary abolitionist of slavery; and Martin Luther King, Jr., unsparing foe of racism.

The prayers of five men of action exemplify that brevity is the soul of wit: Sir Francis Drake, Admiral Nelson, and generals Oliver Cromwell, Sir Jacob Astley, and Charles George Gordon.

Professors, men of reflection, find a place here: Edward Bouverie Pusey and William Bright of Oxford, Edward C. Ratcliffe of Cambridge, John Baillie of Edinburgh, Percy Dearmer of London, William Sperry and Samuel H. Miller (both deans of Harvard University Divinity School), and Gregory Vlastos of Princeton. Two headmasters who wrote prayers of note are included: Thomas Arnold of Rugby School, and Charles S. Martin of St. Alban's School, Washington, D.C. An unlikely profession for devotional creativity is journalism; its single representative is the renowned Malcolm Muggeridge, former editor of *Punch*.

As might be expected, a number of theologians are included—thirteen, to be exact: Origen, St. Augustine, St. Anselm, St. John of Damascus, Abelard, St. Thomas Aquinas, Luther, Calvin, F. D. Maurice, Peter Taylor Forsyth, Reinhold Niebuhr, Teilhard de Chardin, and Dietrich Bonhoeffer. To their number can be added the mystics represented: St. Patrick, St. Columba, St. John of the Cross, Thomas à Kempis, and Johannes Tauler, as well as Mechthild of Magdeburg and Dame Julian of Norwich.

Among the higher ecclesiastics, we have Archbishop Fénelon of Cambrai and Cardinal John Henry Newman, both Catholics. Several who served as archbishop of Canterbury and wrote notable prayers are featured: Thomas Cranmer, William Laud, Edward White Benson, and William Temple, the socialist primate. Anglican bishops include Miles Coverdale, the earliest translator of the Bible into English; Nicholas Ridley, the Protestant martyr; Edward Reynolds, the author of the General Thanksgiving of the Book of Common Prayer; Phillips Brooks, author of the Christmas carol "O Little Town of Bethlehem"; and many others, such as Edward Lambe Parsons of California.

In the procession of the famous you will find some of the great religious leaders and founders: St. Francis of Assisi; St. Ignatius Loyola, founder of the Jesuits; Luther and his friend Melanchthon; John Calvin; the Quaker George Fox; the Methodist John Wesley and Susanna Wesley, his mother; Willem Visser 't Hooft, the first secretary of the World Council of Churches, whose apt name can be translated as "the chief Fisherman"; and a modern saint, Mother Teresa of Calcutta, who contributes four prayers of love and compassion.

The selection of prayers was thoroughly ecumenical, so there are contributions from all major denominational groups: Roman Catholics, Eastern Orthodox, Anglicans, and Protestants. The Baptists contribute the devotions of George Dawson, Charles H. Spurgeon, and Walter Rauschenbusch; the Congregationalists rejoice in Henry Ward Beecher, John Hunter, and J. H. Jowett; the Methodists feature the Wesleys and Leslie D. Weatherhead; the Presbyterians acclaim John Baillie, Henry Sloane Coffin, and William Sloane Coffin, Jr.; and the Reformed include John Calvin and Reinhold Niebuhr. Also featured is Dwight L. Moody, the great American revivalist.

Here in the greatest possible variety are the friends of God with prayers for our heartening, whatever our earthly callings, inviting us to become *their* friends and to follow them only as far as they followed Christ.

III

This volume includes a variety of prayers grouped according to six classifications: (1) prayers of gratitude and dedication; (2) prayers of confession and penitence; (3) prayers of petition; (4) prayers of intercession; (5) prayers marking times; and (6) prayers for the Christian year.

The logic of the order of the prayers is as inevitable as it is natural. We move from gratitude and dedication to God for all the gifts of nature and of grace to confessions of our own unworthiness of such generosity because of our sins against God and our neighbors. With equal inevitability and naturalness, we make our petitions for all the graces of the Christian life that we need to improve ourselves with God's assistance, which ultimately means sanctification. These petitions make up the most comprehensive category, which includes prayers for the graces and virtues of the Christian life—for sanctification, for patience, for courage, for joy and contentment, and so on. From these personal and cleansing concerns, we move out in compassion to remember the needs of others in our prayers of intercession, intercession for the church, the nation, and the city, for workers, for God's creatures, both humans and animals.

Augmenting this cycle are the prayers marking certain times—morning and evening, the hours of dying and death—and the occasions of the Christian year, from Advent and Christmas, through Lent and Easter, to Pentecost and Trinity Sunday.

Overwhelmed as we almost are by such things as spiritual doubts and impoverishment, and the fear of a nuclear holocaust, it is not easy to pray with confidence in the late twentieth century. For these reasons alone, it is imperative that we seek guidance and cheer from the noteworthy people here represented, who were burdened with great responsibilities that were lightened by prayer as they joined in the communion of saints.

Department of Religion   HORTON DAVIES
Princeton University

THE COMMUNION OF SAINTS

PART 1

PRAYERS OF GRATITUDE AND DEDICATION

A. PRAYERS OF GRATITUDE

You have given so much to me,
Give one thing more, a grateful heart.

George Herbert (1593–1633)
Anglican divine and metaphysical poet

Lord God, heavenly Father, we know that we are dear children of yours and that you are our beloved Father, not because we deserve it, nor ever could merit it, but because our dear Lord, your only-begotten Son, Jesus Christ, wills to be our brother, and of his own accord offers and makes this blessing known to us. Since we may consider ourselves his brothers and sisters and he regards us as such, you will permit us to become and remain your children for ever. Amen.

Martin Luther (1483–1546)
The great German reformer

Almighty God, Father of all mercies, we your unworthy servants give you most humble and hearty thanks for all your goodness and loving-kindness to us, and to all. We bless you for our creation, preservation, and all the blessings of this life; but above all, for your inestimable love in the redemption of the world by our Lord Jesus Christ; for the means of grace, and for the hope of glory. And, we beg you, give us that due sense of all your mercies, that our hearts may be unfeignedly thankful, and that we show forth your praise, not only with our lips, but in our lives: by giving up ourselves to your service and by walking before you in holiness and righteousness all our days; through Jesus Christ our Lord, to whom with you and the Holy Spirit be all honor and glory, world without end.

*The General Thanksgiving of the Book of
Common Prayer (1662), composed by
Edward Reynolds (1599–1676)
Bishop of Norwich*

Accept, O Lord God, our Father, the sacrifices of our thanksgiving; this, of praise, for your great mercies already afforded to us; and this, of prayer, for the continuance and enlargement of them; this, of penitence, for such only recompense as our sinful nature can endeavor; and this, of the love of our hearts, as the only gift you ask or desire, and all these, through the all-holy and atoning sacrifice of Jesus Christ your Son our Savior.

*John Donne (1572–1631)
Metaphysical poet and dean of
St. Paul's Cathedral, London*

O eternal and most glorious God. . . . You who assure us that precious in your sight is the death of your saints, enable us in life and death, seriously to consider the value, the price of a soul. It is precious, O Lord, because your image is stamped and imprinted upon it; precious, because the blood of your Son was paid for it; precious, because your blessed Spirit, the Holy Ghost works upon it, and tests it, by his various fires; and precious, because it is entered into your revenue, and made a part of your treasure.

John Donne

O eternal and most gracious God, who made little things to signify great, and conveyed to us the infinite merits of your Son in the water of Baptism, and the Bread and Wine of your other Sacrament, receive the sacrifice of my humble thanks, that you have not only given me the ability to rise out of this bed of weariness and discomfort, but have also made this bodily rising by your grace, a promise of a second resurrection from sin, and of a third, to everlasting glory.

John Donne

O heavenly Father, your hand replenishes all living creatures with blessing and gives meat to the hungry in due season; we acknowledge our meat and drink to be your gifts, prepared by your fatherly providence to be received by us for the comfort of our bodies with thanksgiving: We most humbly beg you to bless us and our food and to give us grace so to use these your benefits that we may be thankful to you and liberal to our poor neighbors, through Jesus Christ our Lord. Amen.

Thomas Becon (c.1511–1567)
Early English reformer

Thanks be to you, Lord Jesus Christ: in all my trials and sufferings you have given me the strength to stand firm; in your mercy you have granted me a share of eternal glory.

Irenaeus of Sirmium, Hungary
(c.120 to 140 – c.200 to 203)
Greek prelate, saint, and martyr

I worship you, Lord; I bless you, God the Good; I beg you, Most Holy; I fall down before you, Lover of humankind.

I give you glory, O Christ, because you, the Only Begotten, the Lord of all things, who alone are without sin, gave yourself to die for me, a sinner unworthy of such a blessing: you died the death of the cross to free my sinful soul from the bonds of sin.

What shall I give you, Lord, in return for all this kindness?

Glory to you for your love.
Glory to you for your mercy.
Glory to you for your patience.
Glory to you for forgiving us all our sins.
Glory to you for coming to save our souls.
Glory to you for your incarnation in the virgin's womb.
Glory to you for your bonds.
Glory to you for receiving the cut of the lash.
Glory to you for accepting mockery.
Glory to you for your crucifixion.
Glory to you for your burial.
Glory to you for your resurrection.
Glory to you that were preached to men and women.
Glory to you in whom they believed.
Glory to you that were taken up into heaven.
Glory to you who sit in great glory at the Father's right hand.
Glory to you whose will it is that the sinner should be saved
through your great mercy and compassion.

St. Ephraim of Syria (c.306–373)
Founder of the Persian School of Edessa

For the sanity of friendship, and the madness of love,
Thanks be to the Lord, our God.

A. S. T. Fisher (1906–1988)
Fellows' chaplain, Magdalen College, Oxford

Make us grateful, O God, for your grace of prayer; whereby we have our conversation in heaven; whereby all impediments are removed, so that nothing can separate us from your goodness, for time and for eternity.

Abbess Gertrude More (1606–1633)
Great-great granddaughter of
Sir Thomas More

Eternal God, my sovereign Lord, I acknowledge all I am, all I have is yours. Give me such a sense of your infinite goodness that I may return to you all possible love and obedience.

John Wesley (1703–1791)
Anglican priest and founder of the
Methodist Church

Blessed are the eyes, O Jesu, that see you in these holy signs; blessed is the mouth that reverently receives you.
Blessed even is the heart that desires your coming.

John Wesley

Be present at our table, Lord;
Be here and everywhere adored.
These creatures bless, and grant that we
May feast in paradise with thee.
Amen.

John Wesley

O God, the true and only life, in whom and from whom and by whom are all good things that are good indeed; from whom to be turned is to fall, to whom to turn is to rise again; in whom to abide is to dwell for ever, from whom to depart is to die; to whom to come again is to revive, and in whom to lodge is to live: take away from me whatever you will as long as you give me only yourself.

Thomas Dekker (c.1570–1632)
English dramatist

We give you thanks, O God, for those who mean so much to us—
   Those to whom we can go at any time.
   Those with whom we can talk and keep nothing back, knowing that they will not laugh at our dreams or our failures.
   Those in whose presence it is easier to be good.
   Those who by their warning have held us back from mistakes we might have made.
   Above all, we thank you for Jesus Christ, Lord of our hearts and Savior of our souls, in whose Name we offer this thanksgiving.

William Barclay (1907–1978)
Professor of New Testament, Glasgow
University, and biblical commentator

O God, we thank you for this universe, our great home; for its vastness and its riches, and for the manifoldness of the life which teems upon it and of which we are part. We praise you for the arching sky and the blessed winds, for the driving clouds and the constellations on high. We praise you for the salt sea and the running water, for the everlasting hills, for the trees, and for the grass under our feet. We thank you for our senses by which we can see the splendor of the morning and hear the jubilant songs of love, and smell the breath of the springtime. Grant us, we pray you, a heart wide open to all this joy and beauty, and save our souls from being so steeped in care or so darkened by passion that we pass heedless and unseeing when even the thornbush by the wayside is aflame with the glory of God. . . .

Walter Rauschenbusch (1861–1918)
American Baptist minister and
exponent of the Social Gospel

Our Father, you are the final source of all our comforts and to you we give thanks for this food. But we also remember in gratitude the many men and women whose labor was necessary to produce it and who gathered it from the land and afar from the sea for our sustenance. Grant that they too may enjoy the fruit of their labor without want, and may be bound up with us in a fellowship of thankful hearts.

Walter Rauschenbusch

I thank you, O God, for the relief and satisfaction of mind that come with the firm assurance that you govern the world; for the patience and resignation to your providence that are afforded as I reflect that even the tumultuous and irregular actions of the sinful are, nevertheless, under your direction, who are wise, good, and

---

omnipotent, and have promised to make all things work together for good to those who love you.

Susanna Wesley (1669–1742)
Mother of 19 children, including John and
Charles Wesley, and author

Some hae meat and canna eat,
And some wad eat that want it;
But we hae meat, and we can eat,
And sae the Lord be thankit.
Amen.

Robert Burns (1759–1796)
Scottish national poet

O God above all, yet in all; holy beyond all imagination, yet Friend of sinners; you inhabit the realms of unfading light, yet lead us through the shadows of mortal life; how solemn and uplifting it is even to think about you. Like sight of sea to wearied eyes, like a walled-in garden to the troubled mind, like home to wanderer, like a strong tower to a soul pursued; so to us is the sound of your Name.

But greater still to feel you in our heart; like a river glorious, cleansing, healing, bringing life; like a song victorious, comforting our sadness, banishing our care; like a voice calling us to battle, urging us beyond ourselves.

But greater far to know you as our Father, as dear as you are near; and ourselves born of your love, made in your image, cared for through all our days, never beyond your sight, never out of your thought.

W. E. Orchard (1877–1955)
Presbyterian minister who became a
Catholic priest and liturgist

When all Thy mercies, O my God,
My rising soul surveys,
Transported with the view, I'm lost,
In wonder, love, and praise.

When worn with sickness, oft hast Thou
With health renewed my face,
And when in sins and sorrows sunk,
Revived my soul with grace.

Ten thousand, thousand precious gifts
My daily thanks employ;
Nor is the least a thankful heart
That takes those gifts with joy.

Through all eternity, to Thee
A grateful song I'll raise;
But O eternity's too short
To utter all thy praise!

Joseph Addison (1672–1719)
English essayist and poet

We thank you for the triumph of truth over error, to us so slow, to yourself so sure. We bless you for every word of truth which has been spoken the wide world through, for all of right which human consciences have perceived and made into institutions.

We thank you for that love which will not stay its hold till it joins all nations and kindreds and tongues and people into one great family of love.

Theodore Parker (1810–1860)
Popular liberal minister (Boston)
and lecturer

To One alone my thoughts arise,
The Eternal Truth, the Good and Wise,
    To Him I cry,
Who shared on earth our common lot,
But the world comprehended not
    His deity.

Henry Wadsworth Longfellow (1807–1882)
American poet

For beauty, Lord, wherever our eyes have seen it, in the heavens or on the earth, in the great seas or tall trees or wide plains, in the flight of birds or the strength of the beasts;

for beauty heard, whether it be in the human voice or the music of manifold instruments fashioned by many skills, whether it be the great sounds of the storm or the laughter of the little child;

for the beauty neither seen nor heard, deeper than the flesh and higher than stars, the grace of the heart's desire and lasting affection, of forgiveness freely given and of hospitality boldly offered, the holiness of saints whose love opens wide, the larger kingdom of the Eternal, and every gesture by which the soul holds high converse with the mystery of your mercy;

for all beauty we bow our hearts gratefully and in reverence and for him in whom life became redeeming grace, even Jesus Christ, we give you thanks. Amen.

Samuel H. Miller (1900–1968)
Dean of Harvard Divinity School
and Baptist minister

O God of mountains, stars, and boundless spaces,
O God of freedom and of joyous hearts,
When you look out from all human faces
There will be room enough in crowded marts!
If you brood around me, then the noise is o'er,
Your universe my closet with shut door.

George MacDonald (1824–1905)
Scottish novelist and Christian apologist

For all the art which thou hast hidden
  In this little piece
    of red clay:
For the workmanship of thy hand,
Who didst thy self form man
Of the dust of the ground,
And breathe into his nostrils
  The breath of Life.
For the high Exaltation whereby thou hast glorified every body,
  Especially mine,
As thou didst thy Servant
  Adam's in Eden.
Thy Works themselves speaking to me the same thing that
    was said
  unto him at the beginning
WE ARE ALL THINE.

Thomas Traherne (1634–1674)
English poet and minister of the
Church of Wales

Let us adore Jesus in our hearts, who spent thirty years out of thirty-three in silence; who began his public life by spending forty days in silence; who often retired alone to spend the night on a mountain in silence. He who spoke with authority, now spends his earthly life in silence. Let us adore Jesus in the eucharistic silence.

Mother Teresa of Calcutta (b. 1910)
Founder of the Sisters of Charity

Praise to the Holiest in the height,
    And in the depths be praise;
In all his words most wonderful,
    Most sure in all his ways. . . .

O loving wisdom of our God!
    When all was sin and shame,
A second Adam to the fight
    And to the rescue came.

O Wisest love! that flesh and blood,
    Which did in Adam fail,
Should strive afresh against the foe,
    Should strive and should prevail;

And that a higher gift than grace
    Should flesh and blood refine;
God's presence and his very self,
    And essence all-divine.

O generous love! that he who smote
    In Man, for man, the foe,
The double agony in Man,
    For man, should undergo;

And in the garden secretly,
  And on the cross on high
Should teach his brethren, and inspire
  To suffer and to die.

Praise to the Holiest in the height,
  And in the depths be praise;
In all his words most wonderful,
  Most sure in all his ways.

John Henry Newman (1801–1890)
Cardinal, theologian, and man of letters

O Lord Jesus Christ, you are the sun of the world, evermore arising, and never going down, which by your most wholesome appearing and sight, brings forth, preserves, nourishes, and refreshes all things, as well that are in heaven as also that are on earth; we beg you mercifully and faithfully to shine in our hearts, so that the night and darkness of sins, and the mists of errors on every side may be driven away; with you brightly shining in our hearts we may all our life space go without stumbling or offense, and may decently and seemly walk (as in the day time), being pure and clean from the works of darkness, and abounding in all good works which God has prepared us to walk in; you who with the Father and with the Holy Ghost live and reign for ever and ever.

Thomas Cranmer (1489–1556)
Archbishop of Canterbury and editor in
chief of the Book of Common Prayer

Almighty and everliving God, we heartily thank you because you feed us, who have received these holy mysteries, with the spiritual food of the most precious Body and Blood of our Savior Jesus Christ, assuring us thereby of your favor and goodness towards us, and that we are members incorporate in his mystical body, the blessed company of all faithful people, and heirs, through hope, of your everlasting kingdom. And we beseech you, heavenly Father, so assist us with your grace, that we may continue in that holy fellowship and do all such good works as you have prepared for us; through the same Jesus Christ our Lord, to whom with you and the Holy Ghost we ascribe all honor and glory, world without end.

Thomas Cranmer

All praise to Him who now hath turned
My fears to joys, my sighs to song,
My tears to smiles, my sad to glad. Amen.

Anne Bradstreet (1612–1672)
New England poet and Puritan

And now unto him who is able to keep us from falling and lift us from the dark valley of despair to the mountains of hope, from the midnight of desperation to the daybreak of joy; to him be power and authority, for ever and ever. Amen.

Martin Luther King, Jr. (1929–1968)
American clergyman and social reformer

B. PRAYERS OF DEDICATION

You awaken us to delight in your praises; for you made us for yourself, and our heart is restless until it reposes in you.

St. Augustine of Hippo (354–430)
First philosopher of Christianity, author of
The Confessions, *and theologian*

Christ, be with me, Christ before me, Christ behind me,
Christ in me, Christ beneath me, Christ above me,
Christ on my right, Christ on my left,
Christ where I lie, Christ where I sit, Christ where I arise,
Christ in the heart of every one who thinks of me,
Christ in every eye that sees me,
Christ in every ear that hears me.
   Salvation is of the Lord,
   Salvation is of the Christ,
   May your salvation, O Lord, be ever with us.

St. Patrick (389–461)
Celtic monk and evangelist of Ireland

Eternal Light, shine into our hearts,
  Eternal Goodness, deliver us from evil;
    Eternal Power, be our support,
Eternal Wisdom, scatter the darkness of our ignorance;
    Eternal Pity, have mercy upon us; that with all our heart
and mind and soul and strength we may seek your face and be
brought by your infinite mercy to your holy presence; Through
Jesus Christ our Lord.

Alcuin of York (c.732–804)
Scholar and Benedictine advisor to
Charlemagne

Almighty God, you who have made all things for us, and us for
your glory, sanctify our body and soul, our thoughts and our
intentions, our words and actions, that whatsoever we shall think,
or speak, or do, may by us be designed to the glorification of your
name . . . and let no pride or self-seeking, no impure motive or
unworthy purpose, no little ends or low imagination stain our
spirit, or profane any of our words and actions. But let our body
be a servant to our spirit, and both body and spirit servants of Jesus
Christ.

Thomas à Kempis (1379–1471)
Dutch mystic, ecclesiastic, and writer

My God,
I pray that I may so know you and love you
    that I may rejoice in you.
And if I may not do so fully in this life
    let me go steadily on
    to the day when I come to that fullness. . . .
    Let me receive
That which you promised through your truth,
    that my joy may be full.

St. Anselm (1033–1109)
Philosopher, archbishop of Canterbury

Take, Lord, all my liberty. Receive my memory, my understanding
and my whole will. Whatever I have and possess, you have given
to me; to you I restore it wholly, and to your will I utterly surrender
it for your direction. Give me the love of you only, with your grace,
and I am rich enough; nor ask I anything beside.

St. Ignatius of Loyola (1491–1556)
Founder of the Society of Jesus and author
of the Spiritual Exercises

Lord, take my heart, for I cannot give it to you. And when you have
it, keep it, for I would not take it from you. And save me in spite
of myself, for Christ's sake.

François de Salignac de La Mothe-Fénelon
(1651–1715)
Archbishop of Cambrai, preacher, and
mystic

Father, into thy hands I give the heart
Which left thee but to learn how good thou art.

George MacDonald (1824–1905)
Scottish novelist and Christian apologist

We have our treasure in earthen vessels, but you, O Holy Spirit, when you live in a man, you live in what is infinitely lower. Spirit of Holiness, you live in the midst of impurity and corruption; Spirit of Wisdom, you live in the midst of folly; Spirit of truth, you live in one who is himself deluded. Oh, continue to dwell there, you who do not seek a desirable dwelling place, for you would seek there in vain, Creator and Redeemer, to make a dwelling for yourself; Oh, continue to dwell there, that one day you may finally be pleased by the dwelling which you prepared in my heart, foolish, deceiving and impure as it is.

Søren Kierkegaard (1813–1855)
Danish philosopher and theologian

Use me, my Savior, for whatever purpose and in whatever way you may require. Here is my poor heart, an empty vessel: fill it with your grace. Here is my sinful and troubled soul: quicken it and refresh it with your love. Take my heart for your abode; my mouth to spread abroad the glory of your name; my love and all my powers for the advancement of your believing people; and never allow the steadfastness and confidence of my faith to abate.

Dwight L. Moody (1837–1899)
American evangelist and educator

Father, I will not ask for wealth or fame,
Though once they would have joyed my carnal sense;
I shudder not to bear a hated name,
Wanting all wealth, myself my sole defense,
But give me, Lord, eyes to behold the truth,
A seeing sense that knows the eternal right;
A heart with pity filled and gentlest ruth;
A valiant faith that makes all darkness light;
Give me the power to labor for mankind;
Make me the mouth of such as cannot speak;
Eyes let me be to groping folk, and blind;
A conscience to the base; and to the weak
Let me be hands and feet; and to the foolish, mind;
And lead still further on such as your kingdom seek.

Theodore Parker (1810–1860)
American clergyman, poet, and lecturer

Before you, Father,
In righteousness and humility,
With you, Brother,
In faith and courage,
In you, Spirit,
In stillness.

Dag Hammarskjöld (1905–1961)
Secretary-General of the United Nations

PART 2

PRAYERS OF CONFESSION AND PENITENCE

Love bade me welcome; yet my soul drew back,
  Guilty of dust and sin.
But quick-eyed Love, observing me grow slack
  From my first entrance in,
Drew nearer to me, sweetly questioning
  If I lacked anything.

"A guest," I answered,"worthy to be here":
  Love said, "You shall be he."
"I, the unkind, ungrateful? Ah my dear,
  I cannot look on Thee."
Love took my hand and smiling did reply,
  "Who made the eyes but I?"

"Truth, Lord, but I have marred them: let my shame
  Go where it doth deserve."
"And know you not," says Love, "Who bore the blame?"
  "My dear, then I will serve."
"You must sit down," says Love, "and taste my meat."
  So I did sit and eat.

George Herbert (1593–1633)
Anglican divine and metaphysical poet
(Simone Weil was converted by this
poem, which she had learned by heart.)

We confess to you, O heavenly Father, as your children and your people, our hardness, and indifference, and impenitence; our grievous failures in your faith and in pure and holy living; our trust in riches and our misuse of them, our confidence in self, through which we daily multiply our own temptations. We confess our timorousness as your Church and witness before the world, and the sin and bitterness that all know in their own hearts. Give us all contrition and meekness of heart, O Father, grace to amend our sinful life, and the holy comfort of your Spirit to overcome and heal all our evils; through Jesus Christ our Lord.

Edward White Benson (1829–1896)
Bishop of Truro, archbishop of
Canterbury

O God of earth and altar,
Bow down and hear our cry,
Our earthly rulers falter,
Our people drift and die;
The walls of gold entomb us,
The swords of scorn divide,
Take not your thunder from us,
But take away our pride!
From all that terror teaches,
From lies of tongue and pen,
From all the easy speeches,
That comfort cruel men,
From sale and profanation
Of honor and the sword,
From sleep and from damnation,
Deliver us, good Lord.

G. K. Chesterton (1874–1936)
English journalist and writer converted to
Catholicism

For this day's sins, O God, grant us mercy:
   for sloth that wasted the hours
   or for haste which outran its benedictions;
   for fear that frustrated bold hopes
   or dullness that took everything for granted;
   for anger that burst forth destructively
   or indifference that smothered the soul;
   for suspicion wrongly held
   or for trust cheaply betrayed;
   for indecision which avoided the evil
   or for compromise which disguised it.

> *Samuel H. Miller (1900–1968)*
> *Dean of Harvard Divinity School*
> *and Baptist minister*

We pray, O Lord, for deliverance from all that weakens faith in you:
   from pompous solemnity;
   from mistaking earnestness for trust in you;
   from seeking easy answers to large questions;
   from being overawed by the self-confident;
   from dependence upon mood and feelings;
   from despondency and the loss of self-respect;
   from timidity and hesitation in making decisions.
In Christ, we pray. Amen.

> *Willard Sperry (1882–1954)*
> *Dean of Harvard Divinity School*
> *and Congregational clergyman*

I am not worthy, Master and Lord, that you should come beneath the roof of my soul: yet, since you in your love toward all wish to dwell in me, in boldness I come. You command, Open the gates—which you alone have forged; and you will come in with love toward all as is your nature; you will come in and enlighten my darkened reason. I believe that you will do this: for you did not send away the harlot that came to you with tears; nor cast out the repentant publican; nor reject the thief who acknowledged your kingdom; nor forsake the repentant persecutor, a yet greater act; but all of those who came to You in repentance, were counted in the band of your friends, who alone abide blessed forever, now, and unto the endless ages.

St. John Chrysostom (c.347–407)
Court preacher in Byzantium and
author of a major liturgy of the
Eastern Orthodox Church

O Jesus, my feet are dirty. Come even as a slave to me, pour water into your bowl, come and wash my feet. In asking such a thing I know I am overbold, but I dread what was threatened when you said to me, "If I do not wash your feet I have no fellowship with you." Wash my feet then, because I long for your companionship. And yet, what am I asking? It was well for Peter to ask you to wash his feet; for him that was all that was needed for him to be clean in every part. With me it is different; though you wash me now I shall still stand in need of that other washing, the cleansing you promised when you said, "there is a baptism I must needs be baptized with."

Origen of Alexandria (c.185–c.254)
First systematic theologian

From needing danger, to be good,
From owing you yesterday's tears today,
    From trusting so much to your blood,
That in that hope, we wound our soul away,
        From bribing you with alms, to excuse
        Some sin more burdenous,
From light affecting, in religion, news,
From thinking us all soul, neglecting thus
Our mutual duties, Lord deliver us.

> *John Donne (1572–1631)*
> *Metaphysical poet and dean of*
> *St. Paul's Cathedral, London*

O think me worth your anger, punish me,
    Burn off my rusts and my deformity.
    Restore your image so much, by your grace,
    That you may know me, and I'll turn my face.

> *John Donne*

O God, early in the morning I cry to you.
Help me to pray
And to concentrate my thoughts on you:
I cannot do this alone.
In me there is darkness,
But with you there is light;
I am lonely, but you do not leave me;
I am feeble in heart, but with you there is help;
I am restless, but with you there is peace.
In me there is bitterness, but with you there is patience;
I do not understand your ways,
But you know the way for me . . . .

Restore me to liberty,
And enable me so to live now
That I may answer before you and before me.
Lord, whatever this day may bring
Your name be praised.

Dietrich Bonhoeffer (1906–1945)
German theologian and anti-Nazi who wrote
this prayer while awaiting execution

Take from us, O God, all tediousness of spirit, all impatience and unquietness. Let us possess ourselves in patience: through Jesus Christ our Lord.

Jeremy Taylor (1613–1667)
English writer and Anglican bishop

Our God, whose Son is the light of the world,
   in his penetrating light we acknowledge our darkness;
   in his constant grace, our careless love;
   in his generous giving, our sordid grasping;
   in his equal justice, our dire prejudice;
   in his fortitude, our fearful failure;
   in his inclusive love, our deep divisions;
   in his pure sacrifice, our soiling sins.
But in his Cross is our forgiveness,
and in his resurrection our enduring hope.
The pardon and the promise now we claim,
in penitence and faith, through Jesus Christ our Lord.

Horton Davies
Professor of Religion,
Princeton University (1956–1984)

PART 3

PRAYERS OF PETITION

A. ARROW PRAYERS

O Lord, you know how busy I must be this day; if I forget you, do not forget me: for Christ's sake.

> *Sir Jacob Astley (1579–1652)*
> *before the battle of Edge Hill in 1642*

O Lord, baptize our hearts into a sense of the conditions and needs of all people.

> *George Fox (1624–1691)*
> *Founder of the Society of Friends*

O God, help us not to despise what we do not understand.

> *William Penn (1644–1718)*
> *Quaker leader and founder of Pennsylvania*

Make us remember, O God, that every day is your gift, to be used according to your command.

> Samuel Johnson (1709–1784)
> English writer and lexicographer

Those things, good Lord, that we pray for,
Give us thy grace to labor for.

> Sir Thomas More (1478–1535)
> Lord chancellor of England and martyr

Teach us to pray often; that we may pray oftener.

> Jeremy Taylor (1613–1667)
> English writer and Anglican bishop

Thy will be done, though in my own undoing.

> Sir Thomas Browne (1605–1682)
> English physician and writer

And so I sometimes think our prayers
    Might well be merged in one;
And nest and perch and hearth and church
    Repeat "Thy will be done!"

> Sir Thomas Browne

PRAYERS OF PETITION

My God, I love you.

The deathbed words of Thérèse of Lisieux
(1873–1897)
French Carmelite nun

O Lord, let us not live to be useless, for Christ's sake. Amen.

John Wesley (1703–1791)
Anglican priest and founder of the
Methodist Church

Pardon, O gracious Jesus, what we have been; with your holy discipline correct what we are.

Order by your providence what we shall be; and in the end, crown your own gifts. Amen.

John Wesley

O God who made this beautiful earth, when will it be ready to receive your saints? How long, O Lord, how long?

George Bernard Shaw (1856–1950)
English dramatist and critic

O Lord, I do not pray for tasks equal to my strength: I ask for strength equal to my tasks.

> *Phillips Brooks (1835–1893)*
> *Episcopal bishop of Massachusetts, author*
> *of the carol "O Little Town of Bethlehem"*

O Lord, deliver us from the need to build ourselves up by cutting others down.

> *Ernest T. Campbell (b. 1915)*
> *Minister of Riverside Church, New York City*

From silly devotions
and from sour-faced saints,
good Lord, deliver us.

> *St. Teresa of Ávila (1515–1582)*
> *Carmelite nun, founder of numerous*
> *convents and monasteries, and author of*
> *several spiritual classics*

Keep us, Lord, so awake in the duties of our callings that we may sleep in your peace and wake in your glory.

> *John Donne (1572–1631)*
> *Metaphysical poet and dean of*
> *St. Paul's Cathedral, London*

O Lord Jesus Christ . . . save us from the error of wishing to admire you instead of being willing to follow you and to resemble you.

Søren Kierkegaard (1813–1855)
Danish philosopher and theologian

Especially we pray you to make Christianity more Christian.

Harry Emerson Fosdick (1878–1969)
First minister of Riverside Church,
  New York City

Lord, take, take my lips and speak through them, take my mind and think through it, take my heart and set it on fire for love of you.

Attributed to W. H. Aitken (1841–1927)
Canon residentiary of
  Norwich Cathedral

Holy Spirit
think through me
till your ideas
are my ideas.

Amy Carmichael (1868–1951)
Anglican missionary and author of
  numerous devotional books and poems

B. PETITIONS FOR THE GRACES AND VIRTUES OF THE CHRISTIAN LIFE

1. For the Guidance and Grace of God

Blessed are all your saints, O God and King, who have traveled over the tempestuous sea of this life and have made the harbor of peace and felicity. Watch over us who are still on our dangerous voyage; and remember those who lie exposed to the rough storms of trouble and temptations. Frail is our vessel, and the ocean is wide; but as in your mercy you have set our course, so steer the vessel of our life towards the everlasting shore of peace, and bring us at length to the quiet haven of our heart's desire, where you, O God, are blessed and live and reign for ever.

St. Augustine of Hippo (354–430)
First philosopher of Christianity, author of
The Confessions, *and theologian*

O you, from whom to be turned is to fall,
   to whom to be turned is to rise,
   and in whom to stand is to abide for ever:
Grant us in all our duties your help
   in all our perplexities your guidance,
   in all our dangers your protection,
   and in all our sorrows your peace;
through Jesus Christ our Lord.

St. Augustine of Hippo

O Lord Jesus Christ, when on earth you were ever occupied about your Father's business; grant that we may not grow weary in well-doing. Give us grace to do all in your name; be the beginning and the end of all; the pattern whom we follow, the Redeemer in whom we trust, the master whom we serve, the friend to whom we look for sympathy. . . . Bring us at last into the eternal presence, where with the Father and the Holy Ghost you live and reign for ever.

Edward Bouverie Pusey (1800–1882)
Canon of Christ Church and regius
professor of Hebrew, Oxford University

O merciful God, fill our hearts, we pray you, with the graces of your Holy Spirit, with love, joy, peace, long-suffering, gentleness, goodness, faith, meekness, temperance. Teach us to love those who hate us; to pray for those who despitefully use us; that we may be your children, our Father, who make your sun to shine on the evil and on the good and send rain on the just and on the unjust.

St. Anselm (1033–1109)
Philosopher, archbishop of Canterbury

O Lord Jesus Christ, you are the Way, the Truth and the Life. We pray you allow us never to stray from you, who are the Way, nor distrust you, who are the Truth, nor to rest in any one other thing than you, who are the Life. Teach us, by your Holy Spirit, what to believe, what to do, and how to take our rest.

Desiderius Erasmus (c.1466–1536)
Dutch humanist, first modern
translator of the New Testament

View me, Lord, a work of Thine:
Shall I then lie drown'd in night?
Might Thy grace in me but shine,
I should seem made all of light.

. . . .

Worldly joys like shadows fade,
When the heav'nly light appears;
But the cov'nants Thou hast made,
Endless, know nor days, nor years.

In Thy word, Lord, is my trust,
To Thy mercies fast I fly;
Though I am but clay and dust,
Yet Thy grace can lift me high.

Thomas Campion (1567–1610)
English poet and composer

O Lord, the Governor of all things, set bounds to our passions by reason, to our errors by truth, to our discontents by good laws justly executed, and to our divisions by charity; that we may be, as your Jerusalem, a country at unity in itself. Grant this, O God, in your good time and for ever; for Christ's sake.

O Lord, make your way plain before me. Let your glory be my end, your Word my rule; and then your will be done.

Charles I (1600–1649)
King of England

Guide me, O Lord, in all the changes and varieties of the world; that in all things that shall happen, I may have an evenness and tranquility of spirit; that my soul may be wholly resigned to your divinest will and pleasure, never murmuring at your gentle chastisements and fatherly correction. Amen.

Jeremy Taylor (1613–1667)
English writer and Anglican bishop

O Lord my God! the amazing horrors of darkness were gathered round me, and covered me all over, and I saw no way to go forth; I felt the depth and extent of the misery of my fellow-creatures separated from the Divine harmony, and it was heavier than I could bear, and I was crushed down under it; I lifted my hand, I stretched out my arm, but there was none to help me; I looked round about, and was amazed. In the depths of misery, O Lord, I remembered that thou art omnipotent; that I had called thee Father; and I felt that I loved thee, and I was made quiet in my will, and I waited for deliverance from thee. Thou had pity on me, when no person could help me; I saw that meekness under suffering was showed to us in the most affecting example of thy Son, and thou taught me to follow him, and I said, "Thy will, O Father, be done!"

John Woolman (1720–1772)
American Quaker and abolitionist

O Lord, come quickly and reign on thy throne, for now often something rises up within me, and tries to take possession of thy throne; pride, covetousness, uncleanness, and sloth want to be my kings; and then evil-speaking, anger, hatred, and the whole train of vices join with me in warring against myself, and try to reign over me. I resist them, I cry out against them, and say, "I have no other king than Christ." O King of Peace, come and reign in me, for I will have no king but thee! Amen.

Bernard of Clairvaux (1090–1153)
Cistercian monk and preacher of
the Crusades

O God, whose eternal providence has embarked our souls in our bodies, not to expect any port of anchorage on the sea of this world, to steer directly through it to your glorious kingdom, preserve us from the dangers that on all sides assault us, and keep our affections still fitly disposed to receive your holy inspirations, that being carried strongly forward by your Holy Spirit we may happily arrive at last in the haven of eternal salvation, through our Lord Jesus Christ.

John Wesley (1703–1791)
Anglican priest and founder of the
Methodist Church

Fix our steps, O Lord, that we may not stagger at the uneven motions of the world, but steadily go on to our glorious home, neither censuring our journey by the weather we meet with, nor turning out of the way by anything that befalls us. . . . Through Jesus Christ our Lord.

John Wesley

O Lord, let nothing divert our advance towards you, but in this dangerous labyrinth of the world and the whole course of our pilgrimage here, your heavenly dictates be our map and your holy life be our guide.

John Wesley

Lead, kindly Light, amid the encircling gloom,
    Lead Thou me on;
The night is dark and I am far from home,
    Lead Thou me on;
Keep Thou my feet: I do not ask to see
The distant scene; one step's enough for me.

I was not ever thus, nor prayed that Thou
    Shouldst lead me on;
I loved to choose and see my path; but now
    Lead Thou me on;
I loved the garish day, and, spite of fears,
Pride rules my will. Remember not past years.

So long Thy power hath blessed me, sure it still
    Will lead me on
O'er moor and fen, o'er crag and torrent, till
    The night is gone;
And with the morn those angel faces smile
Which I have loved long since, and lost awhile.

John Henry Newman (1801–1890)
Cardinal, theologian, and man of letters

May the strength of God pilot us. May the power of God preserve us. May the wisdom of God instruct us. May the hand of God protect us. May the way of God direct us. May the shield of God defend us.

St. Patrick (389–461)
Celtic monk and evangelist of Ireland

We trust in the great Disposer of all events, and in the justice of our cause. I thank God for this great opportunity of doing my duty.

Lord Nelson (1758–1805)
English admiral

O Creator past all telling,
You have appointed from the treasures of your wisdom
the hierarchies of angels,
disposing them in wondrous order above the bright heavens,
and have so beautifully set out all parts of the universe.
You we call the true fount of wisdom
and the noble origin of all things.
Be pleased to shed on the darkness of mind in which I was born,
the twofold beam of your light
and warmth to dispel my ignorance and sin.
You make eloquent the tongues of children.
Then instruct my speech and touch my lips with graciousness.
Make me keen to understand, quick to learn,
able to remember;
make me delicate to interpret and ready to speak.
Guide my going in and going forward,
lead home my going forth.
You are true God and true man, and live for ever and ever.

St. Thomas Aquinas (1225–1274)
Dominican philosophical theologian

Give me, O Lord,
A steadfast heart, which no unworthy affection may drag downwards;
Give me an unconquered heart, which no tribulation can wear out;
Give me an upright heart, which no unworthy purpose may tempt aside.

St. Thomas Aquinas

Do you, my God, stand by me, against all the world's wisdom and reason. . . . Not mine but yours is the cause. . . . I would prefer to have peaceful days and to be out of this turmoil. But yours, O Lord, is this cause; it is righteous and eternal. Stand by me, you true Eternal God! In no man do I trust. . . . Stand by me, O God, in the name of your dear Son Jesus Christ, who shall be my Defense and Shelter, yes, my Mighty Fortress, through the might and strength of your Holy Spirit. Amen.

Martin Luther (1483–1546)
The great German reformer

Lord, we pray not for tranquility, nor that our tribulations may cease; we pray for your spirit and your love, that you grant us strength and grace to overcome adversity; through Jesus Christ. Amen.

Girolamo Savonarola (1452–1498)
Dominican preacher and Florentine
reformer

Grant, O Lord, that we may live in your fear, die in your favor, rest in your peace, rise in your power, reign in your glory; for the sake of your Son, Jesus Christ our Lord. Amen.

William Laud (1573–1645)
Bishop of London, archbishop
of Canterbury

O Lord, by all your dealings with us, whether of joy or pain, of light or darkness, let us be brought to you. Let us value no treatment of your grace simply because it makes us happy or because it makes us sad, because it gives us or denies us what we want; but may all that you send us bring us to you; that knowing your perfectness, we may be sure in every disappointment you are still loving us, in every darkness you are still enlightening us, and in every enforced idleness you are giving us life, as in his death you gave life to your Son, our Savior, Jesus Christ. Amen.

Phillips Brooks (1835–1893)
Episcopal bishop of Massachusetts, author
of the carol "O Little Town of Bethlehem"

Lord, bless us, if it may be, in all our innocent endeavors. If it may not, give us the strength to encounter what is to come, that we be brave in peril, constant in tribulation, temperate in wrath and in all changes of fortune, and, down to the gates of death, loyal and loving one to another. As the clay to the potter, as the windmill to the wind, as children of their sire, we beg of you this help and mercy for Christ's sake.

Robert Louis Stevenson (1850–1894)
Scottish essayist, novelist, and poet

PRAYERS OF PETITION

Lord God almighty,
I pray you for your great mercy and by the token of the
    Holy Cross,
Guide me to your will, to my soul's need, better than I can
    myself;
And shield me against my foes, seen and unseen;
And teach me to do your will
    that I may inwardly love you before all things with a clean mind
    and a clean body.
For you are my maker and my redeemer,
    my help, my comfort, my trust, and my hope.
Praise and glory be to you, now, ever and ever, world without
    end.

> *Alfred the Great (849–899)*
> *King of England*

2. For Divine Mercy and Love

To Mercy, Pity, Peace, and Love,
All pray in their distress;
And to these virtues of delight
Return their thankfulness.

For Mercy, Pity, Peace, and Love,
Is God our Father dear,
And Mercy, Pity, Peace, and Love
Is Man, His child and care.

> *William Blake (1757–1827)*
> *English poet, painter, and mystic*

Show me, O Lord, your mercy, and delight my heart with it. Let me find you whom I so longingly seek. See, here is the man whom the robbers seized, mishandled, and left half dead on the road to Jericho. O kind-hearted Samaritan, come to my aid! I am the sheep who wandered into the wilderness—seek after me, and bring me home again to your fold. Do with me what you will, that I may stay by you all the days of my life, and praise you with all those who are with you in heaven for all eternity.

St. Jerome (c.347–420)
Biblical scholar and hermit

I beg you, O Lord, that the fiery and sweet strength of your love may absorb my soul away from all things that are under heaven, that I may die for love of your love as you deigned to die for love of my love.

St. Francis of Assisi (1181–1226)
Founder of the Franciscan orders

O eternal God . . . let me, in spite of me, be of so much use to your glory, that by your mercy to my sin, other sinners may see how much sin you can pardon.

John Donne (1572–1631)
Metaphysical poet and dean of
St. Paul's Cathedral, London

God, of your goodness, give me yourself; for you are sufficient for me. I cannot properly ask anything less, to be worthy of you. If I were to ask less, I should always be in want. In you alone do I have all.

Julian of Norwich
(1342–after 1416)
English mystic

O Lord God! I trusted in you;
O my beloved Jesus! Free me now;
In callous chains, in penalty's pains,
I long for you.
Fainting, searching and genuflecting
I adore you and implore you to free me.

Mary, Queen of Scots (1542–1587)

I pray, O Master, that the flames of Hell may not touch me nor any of those whom I love, and even that they may never touch anyone (and I know, my God, that you will forgive this bold prayer). . . .

Teilhard de Chardin (1881–1955)
French Jesuit, paleontologist, and
philosopher

O shine upon me, blessed Lord,
Ev'n for my Savior's sake;
In Thee alone is more than all,
And there content I'll take.

Anne Bradstreet (1612–1672)
New England poet and Puritan

3. For Total Obedience

O eternal God, you commit to us the swift and solemn trust of life; since we do not know what a day may bring forth, but only that the hour for serving you is ever present, may we wake to the instant claims of your holy will, not waiting for tomorrow, but yielding today. Lay to rest, by the persuasion of your Spirit, the resistance of our passion, our indolence, or our fear. Consecrate with your presence the way in which our feet may go; and the humblest work will shine, and the roughest places be made plain. Lift us above unrighteous anger and mistrust into faith and hope and charity by a simple and steadfast reliance on your sure will. In all things draw us to the mind of Christ, that your lost image may be traced again and that you may own us as at one with him and you. Amen.

James Martineau (1805–1900)
English Unitarian minister and
theologian

O, dear Savior, be not impatient with us, but still school us at your feet, till at last we shall have learned some of the sublime lessons of self-sacrifice, of meekness, humility, fervor, boldness, and love which your life is fit to teach us. O Lord, we beg you, mold us into your own image. Let us live in you and live like you.

Charles H. Spurgeon (1834–1892)
English Baptist minister and
biblical expositor

Lord, educate us for a higher life, and let that life be begun here. May we be always in the school, always disciples, and when we are out in the world may we be trying to put into practice what we have learned at Jesus' feet. What he tells us in darkness may we proclaim in the light, and what he whispers in our ear in the closets may we sound forth upon the house-tops.

Charles H. Spurgeon

God of all goodness, grant us to desire ardently, to seek wisely, to know surely, and to accomplish perfectly your holy will, for the glory of your name. Amen.

St. Thomas Aquinas (1225–1274)
Dominican philosophical theologian

O Lord our God, grant us grace to desire you with a whole heart, that so desiring you we may seek and find you, and so finding you may love you, and loving you may hate those sins which separate us from you, for the sake of Jesus Christ. Amen.

St. Anselm (1033–1109)
Philosopher, archbishop of Canterbury

O Lord, let me not henceforth desire health or life, except to spend them for you, with you, and in you. You alone know what is good for me; do, therefore, what seems best to you. Give to me, or take from me; conform my will to yours; and grant that, with humble and perfect submission, and in holy confidence, I may receive the orders of your eternal Providence; and may equally adore all that comes to me from you; through Jesus Christ our Lord. Amen.

Blaise Pascal (1623–1662)
French philosopher, mathematician,
*   and mystic*

Govern all by your wisdom, O Lord, so that my soul may always be serving you as you will, and not as I may choose. Do not punish me, I beg you, by granting what I wish or ask, if it offends your love which should always live in me. Let me die to myself, that so I may serve you: let me live for you, who in yourself are the true life.

St. Teresa of Ávila (1515–1582)
Carmelite nun, founder of numerous
*   convents and monasteries, and author of*
*   several spiritual classics*

O God, the Father of the forsaken, the help of the weak, the supplier of the needy, you have diffused and proportioned your gifts to body and soul, in such sort that all may acknowledge and perform the joyous duty of mutual service; you teach us that love towards the human race is the bond of perfection, and the imitation of your blessed self; open our eyes and touch our hearts, that we may see and do, both for this world and for that which is to come, the things which belong unto our peace. Strengthen me in the work I have undertaken; give me counsel and wisdom, perseverance, faith and zeal, and in your own good time, and according to your pleasure, prosper the issue. Pour into me a spirit of humility; let nothing be done but in devout obedience to your will, thankfulness for your unspeakable mercies, and love to your adorable Son Christ Jesus. Amen.

Anthony Ashley Cooper (1801–1885)
Seventh earl of Shaftesbury, English
philanthropist

Speak, Lord, for Thy servant heareth.
Grant us ears to hear,
Eyes to see,
Wills to obey,
Hearts to love;
Then declare what Thou wilt,
Reveal what Thou wilt,
Command what Thou wilt,
Demand what Thou wilt.

Christina Rossetti (1830–1894)
English poet

You who are unchangeable, whom nothing changes! You who are unchangeable in love, precisely for our welfare not submitting to any change: may we too will our welfare, submitting ourselves to the discipline of your unchangeableness, so that we may in unconditional obedience find our rest and remain at rest in unchangeableness.

Søren Kierkegaard (1813–1855)
Danish philosopher and theologian

O Lord, my best desire fulfill,
    And help me to resign
Life, health, and comfort, to your will,
    And make your pleasure mine.

William Cowper (1731–1800)
English poet

We most humbly beg you to give us grace not only to be hearers of the Word, but doers also of the same; not only to love, but also to live your gospel; not only to favor, but also to follow your godly doctrine; not only to profess, but also to practice your blessed commandments, to the honor of your Holy Name, and the health of our souls.

Thomas Becon (c.1511–1567)
Early English reformer

O God, stay with me; let no word cross my lips that is not your word, no thoughts enter my mind that are not your thoughts, no deed ever be done or entertained by me that is not your deed.

Malcolm Muggeridge (b. 1903)
Journalist and agnostic turned Christian

Do I ask any faculty highest, to image success?
I but open my eyes —and perfection, no more and no less,
In the kind I imagined, full-fronts me, and God is seen God
In the star, in the stone, in the flesh, in the soul and the clod.
And thus within and around me I ever renew
(with that stoop of the soul which in bending upraises it too)
The submission of man's nothing—perfect to God's all—
     complete,
As by each new obeisance in spirit, I climb to his feet.

Robert Browning (1812–1889)
English poet

Lord, since you have taken from me all that I had from you, yet of your grace leave me the gift which every dog has by nature: that of being true to you in my distress, when I am deprived of all consolation. This I desire more fervently than your heavenly kingdom!

Mechthild of Magdeburg (c.1210–c.1280)
German nun and mystic

4. For Reverence

Teach us, O Lord, to fear you without being afraid; to fear you in love that we may love you without fear.

Christina Rossetti (1830–1894)
English poet

O Lord and Master of us all;
Whate'er our name or sign,
We own thy sway, we hear thy call,
We test our lives by thine.

John Greenleaf Whittier (1807–1892)
American poet

O God of interstellar space, in whose sight a thousand years are as an evening gone; enlarge our horizons, we beg you, that we may behold your majesty in all your works and know your lordship in all your ways.

Robert N. Rodenmayer (1909–1979)
American Episcopal priest and anthologist

O Lord God, grant us always, whatever the world may say, to content ourselves with what you will say, and to care only for your approval, which will outweigh all worlds; for Jesus Christ's sake.

Charles George Gordon (1833–1885)
British colonial administrator

Grant, O Lord God, that we may wait anxiously, as servants standing in the presence of their Lord, for the least hint of your will; that we may welcome all truth, under whatever outward forms it be uttered; that we may have grace to receive new thoughts with grace, recognizing that your ways are not as our ways, nor your thoughts as our thoughts; that we may bless every good deed by whomsoever it may be done; that we may rise above all party strife and cries to the contemplation of the eternal truth and goodness, O God almighty who never changes; through your Son, our Savior Jesus Christ.

Ascribed to Charles Kingsley (1819–1875)
Anglican clergyman, novelist, and
Christian Socialist

He whom I bow to only knows to whom I bow
When I attempt the ineffable Name, murmuring *Thou,*
And dream of Pheidian fancies and embrace in heart
Symbols (I know) which cannot be the thing thou art.
Thus always, taken at their word, all prayers blaspheme
Worshipping with frail images a folk-lore dream,
And all men in their praying, self-deceived, address
The coinage of their own unquiet thoughts, unless
Thou in magnetic mercy to thyself divert
Our arrows aimed unskillfully, beyond desert;
And all men are idolators, crying unheard
To a deaf idol, if thou take them at their word.

Take not, O Lord, our literal sense. Lord, in thy great,
Unbroken speech our limping metaphor translate.

C. S. Lewis (1898–1963)
Oxford don, Cambridge professor,
Christian apologist

5. For Faith and Confidence in God

Almighty God, Lord of the storm and of the calm, the vexed sea and the quiet haven, of day and of night, of life and of death, grant unto us so to have our hearts stayed upon your faithfulness, your unchangingness and love, that, whatsoever betide us, however black the cloud or dark the night, with quiet faith trusting in you we may look upon you with untroubled eye, and walking in lowliness towards you, and in lovingness towards another, abide all storms and troubles of this mortal life, begging you that they may turn to the soul's true good. We ask it for your mercy's sake, shown in Jesus Christ our Lord.

George Dawson (1821–1876)
English Baptist minister and founder of the
Church of our Saviour, Birmingham

O most loving Father, you who will us to give thanks for all things, to dread nothing but the loss of yourself, and to cast all our care on you, who care for us; Preserve us from faithless fears and worldly anxieties, and grant that no clouds of this mortal life may hide from us the light of that love which is immortal, and which you have manifested unto us in your Son, Jesus Christ our Lord.

William Bright (1824–1901)
Hymnwriter and professor of ecclesiastical
history, Oxford University

O Lord God, in whom we live and move and have our being, open our eyes that we may behold your fatherly presence ever about us. Teach us to be anxious for nothing, and when we have done what you have given us to do, help us, O God our Savior, to leave the issue to your wisdom, knowing that all things are possible to us through your Son our Savior, Jesus Christ.

Richard Meux Benson (1824–1915)
Founder of the Anglican Society of Mission
Priests of St. John the Evangelist

Almighty and everliving God, who for the confirmation of the faith, allowed your holy apostle Thomas to be doubtful of your Son's resurrection: grant us so perfectly, and without all doubt, to believe in your Son Jesus Christ, that our faith in your sight may never be reproved. Hear us, O Lord, through the same Jesus Christ, to whom, with you and the Holy Spirit, be all honor and glory, now and for ever more. Amen.

Thomas Cranmer (1489–1556)
Archbishop of Canterbury and editor in
chief of the Book of Common Prayer

O God in heaven, have mercy on us! Lord Jesus Christ, intercede for your people, deliver us at the opportune time, preserve in us the true genuine Christian faith, collect your scattered sheep with your voice, your divine Word as Holy Writ calls it. Help us to recognize your voice, help us not to be allured by the madness of the world, so that we may never fall away from you, O Lord Jesus Christ.

Albrecht Dürer (1471–1528)
German painter and engraver

O Lord, you who are all merciful, take away my sins from me, and enkindle within me the fire of your Holy Spirit. Take away this heart of stone from me, and give me a heart of flesh and blood, a heart to love and adore you, a heart which may delight in you, love you and please you, for Christ's sake.

St. Ambrose (339–397)
Bishop of Milan

Father in heaven, draw our hearts to you, that our hearts may be where our treasures ought to be, that our minds and thoughts may look to your kingdom, whose citizens we are. Thus, when you shall call us hence, our departure may not be a painful separation from this world, but a joyous meeting with you. Perhaps a long road still lies before us. Yet sometimes our strength is taken from us, and a faintness overcomes us, like a mist before our eyes, so that we are in the darkness of the night; restless desires stir within us, impatient, wild longings, and the heart groans in anxious anticipation of what is to come: O Lord our God, do teach us then, and strengthen in our hearts the conviction that in life as in death we belong to you.

Søren Kierkegaard (1813–1855)
Danish philosopher and theologian

Father, in heaven! You have loved us first; help us never to forget that you are love so that this sure conviction might triumph in our hearts over the seduction of the world, over the disquiet of the soul, over the anxiety for the future, over the fright of the past, over the distress of the moment. But grant also that this conviction might discipline our soul so that our heart might remain faithful and sincere in the love which we bear to all those whom you have commanded us to love as we love ourselves.

Søren Kierkegaard

Grant, O heavenly Father, that we so faithfully believe in you and so fervently love one another, always living in your fear, and in the obedience of your holy law and blessed will, that we, being fruitful in all good works, may lead our life according to your good pleasure in this transitory world and, after this frail and short life, obtain the true and immortal life, where you live and reign, world without end. Amen.

Thomas Becon (c.1511–1567)
Early English reformer

We desire, O Lord, that you will, to all your other mercies, add that gift by which we shall trust in you—faith that works by love; faith that abides with us; faith that transforms material things, and gives them to us in spiritual meanings; faith that illumines the world by a light that never sets, that shines brighter than the day, and that clears the night quite out of our experience. . . . We beg you to grant us this faith, that shall give us victory over the world and over ourselves; that shall make us valiant in all temptation and bring us off conquerors and more than conquerors through him that loved us. Amen.

Henry Ward Beecher (1813–1887)
American Congregational minister and
social reformer

O living Will that shall endure
  When all that seems shall suffer shock,
  Rise in the spiritual rock,
Flow thro' our deeds and make them pure,

That we may lift from out of dust
   A voice as unto him who hears,
   A cry above the conquer'd years
To One that with us works, and trust,

With faith that comes of self-control,
   The truths that never can be proved
   Until we close with all we loved,
And all we flow from, soul in soul.

Alfred, Lord Tennyson (1809–1892)
English poet

Lord, why should I doubt any more, when you have given me such assured pledges of your love? First, you are my Creator, I am your creature, you my Master, I your servant. But hence arises not my comfort: you are my Father, I am your child. "You shall be my sons and daughters," says the Lord almighty. Christ is my brother: "I ascend to my Father and your Father, to my God and your God; but, lest this should not be enough, your maker is your husband." Nay, more, I am a member of his body, he my head. Such privileges—had not the Word of truth made them known, who or where is the man that dared in his heart have presumed to have thought it? So wonderful are these thoughts that my spirit fails in me at their consideration, and I am confounded to think that God, who has done so much for me, should have so little from me. But this is my comfort, that when I come to heaven, I shall understand perfectly what he has done for me, and then I shall be able to praise him as I ought. Lord, having this hope, let me purify myself as you are pure, and let me be no more afraid of death, but even desire to be dissolved and be with you, which is best of all.

Anne Bradstreet (c.1612–1672)
New England poet and Puritan

Grant, almighty God, that as you have, in various ways, testified and daily also prove how dear and precious to you is humanity as we enjoy daily so many and so remarkable proofs of your goodness and favor—O grant that we learn to rely wholly on your goodness, so many examples of which you set before us, and which you would have us continually to experience, that we may not only pass through our earthly course, but also confidently aspire to the hope of that blessed and celestial life which is laid up for us in heaven, through Christ alone our Lord. Amen.

John Calvin (1509–1564)
French theologian and reformer
in Geneva

6. For Truth and Truthfulness

Almighty God, who sent the Spirit of truth to us to guide us into all truth: so rule our lives by your power that we may be truthful in thought and word and deed. May no fear or hope ever make us false in act or speech; cast out from us whatsoever loves or makes a lie, and bring us all into the perfect freedom of your truth, through Jesus Christ our Lord.

Brooke Foss Westcott (1825–1901)
Bishop of Durham, biblical scholar

Holy Spirit of God, who prefers before all temples the upright heart and pure, instruct us in all truth; what is dark, illumine; what is low, raise and support; what is shallow, deepen; that every chapter in our lives may witness to your power and justify the ways of God to men. In the name of Jesus, giver of all grace. Amen.

John Milton (1608–1674)
English poet

God grant me—
The serenity to accept the things I cannot change,
The courage to change the things I can,
And the wisdom to distinguish the one from the other.

Reinhold Niebuhr (1892–1971)
Professor of Applied Christian Ethics,
Union Theological Seminary, New York

Almighty and everliving God, you are beyond the grasp of our highest thought, but within the reach of our frailest trust: Come in the beauty of the morning's light and reveal yourself to us. Enrich us out of the heritage of seers and scholars and saints into whose faith and labors we have entered, and quicken us to new insights for our time; that we may be possessors of the truth of many yesterdays, partakers of your thoughts for today, and creators with you of a better tomorrow; through Jesus Christ, the Lord of the ages.

Henry Sloane Coffin (1877–1954)
Minister of Madison Avenue Presbyterian
Church and president of Union
Theological Seminary, New York

You, O eternal Trinity, are a deep sea, into which the more I enter the more I find, and the more I find the more I seek. The soul cannot be satiated in your abyss, for she continually hungers after you, the eternal Trinity, desiring to see you with the light of your light. As the hart desires the springs of living water, so my soul desires to leave the prison of this dark body and see you in truth.

O abyss, O eternal Godhead, O sea profound, what more could you give me than yourself? You are the fire that ever burns without being consumed; you consume in your heat all the soul's self-love; you are the fire which takes away cold; with your light you illuminate me so that I may know all your truth. Clothe me, clothe me with yourself, eternal truth, so that I may run this mortal life with true obedience, and with the light of your most holy faith.

> *Catherine of Siena (1347–1380)*
> *Dominican nun and consultant to popes*

O God, be present with me in my studies and enquiries.

Grant, O Lord, that I may not lavish away the life which you have given me on useless trifles, nor waste it in vain searches after the things which you have hidden from me.

Enable me, by your Holy Spirit . . . to obtain in all my undertakings such success as will most promote your glory and the salvation of my own soul, for the sake of Jesus Christ. Amen.

> *Samuel Johnson (1702–1784)*
> *English writer and lexicographer*

7. For the Illumination and Power of the Holy Spirit

Enlighten us, O God, by your Spirit, in the understanding of your Word, and grant us the grace to receive it in true fear and humility, that we may learn to put our trust in you, to fear and honor you, by glorifying your Holy Name in all our life, and to yield you the love and obedience which faithful servants owe to their master and children to their fathers, seeing it has led you to call us to the number of your servants and children.

John Calvin (1509–1564)
French theologian and reformer in Geneva

May the Lord grant that we may engage in contemplating the mysteries of his heavenly wisdom with really increasing devotion, to his glory and our edification. Amen.

John Calvin

O gracious and holy Father,
Give us wisdom to perceive you,
intelligence to understand you,
diligence to seek you,
patience to wait for you,
eyes to see you,
a heart to meditate on you,
and a life to proclaim you,
through the power of the Spirit of Jesus Christ our Lord.

St. Benedict (480–547)
Founder of Western Christian monasticism

Because we have need continually to crave many things at your hands, we humbly beg you, O heavenly Father, to grant us your Holy Spirit to direct our petitions, that they may proceed from such a fervent mind as may be agreeable to your holy will. Amen.

John Knox (1513–1572)
Scottish reformer

O God our Father, who sent your Son to be our Savior: renew in us day by day the power of your Holy Spirit; that with knowledge and zeal, with courage and love, with gratitude and hope, we may strive powerfully in your service: may he keep our vision clear, our aspiration high, our purpose firm and our sympathy wide; that we may live as faithful soldiers and servants of our Lord Jesus Christ.

William Temple (1881–1944)
Archbishop of Canterbury and president of
the Workers' Educational Association

O gracious Father, keep me through your Holy Spirit; keep my heart soft and tender now in health and amidst the bustle of the world; keep the thought of yourself present to me as my father in Jesus Christ; and keep alive in me a spirit of love and meekness to all, that I may be at once gentle and active and firm. O strengthen me to bear pain or sickness, or danger, or whatever you shall be pleased to lay upon me, as Christ's soldier and servant; and let my faith overcome the world daily. Perfect and bless the works of your Spirit in the hearts of all your people, and may your kingdom come and your will be done in earth as it is in heaven.

Thomas Arnold (1795–1842)
Headmaster of Rugby School and father of
Matthew Arnold

Almighty and Holy Spirit, the comforter, pure, living, true—illumine, govern, sanctify me, and confirm my heart and mind in the faith, and in all genuine consolation; preserve and rule over me so that, dwelling in the house of the Lord, all the days of my life, I may behold the Lord and praise him with a joyful spirit, and in union with all the heavenly Church. Amen.

Philipp Melanchthon (1497–1560)
German scholar and reformer

O heavenly Father, the author and fountain of all truth, the bottomless sea of all understanding, send, we beg you, your Holy Spirit into our hearts, and lighten our understandings with the beams of your heavenly grace. We ask this, O merciful Father, for your dear Son, our Savior, Jesus Christ's sake. Amen.

Nicholas Ridley (c.1503–1555)
Bishop of London and Marian martyr

Holy Spirit, truth divine,
Dawn upon this soul of mine;
Word of God and inward light,
Wake my spirit, clear my sight.

Holy Spirit, love divine,
Glow within this heart of mine,
Kindle every high desire,
Purge me now in thy pure fire.

Holy Spirit, peace divine,
Still this restless heart of mine,
Speak to calm this tossing sea,
Stayed in thy tranquility.

Holy Spirit, joy divine,
Gladden thou this heart of mine;
In the desert ways I'll sing,
Spring, O well, for ever spring.

Samuel Longfellow (1819–1892)
American hymnwriter

Thou, O Spirit, that dost prefer
Before all temples the upright heart and pure,
Instruct me for thou know'st; thou from the first
Wast present, and, with mighty wings outspread,
Dove-like, sat'st brooding on the vast abyss,
And mad'st it pregnant.

John Milton (1608–1674)
English poet

Creator Spirit, by whose aid
The world's foundations first were laid,
Come, visit every pious mind;
Come, pour thy joys on humankind;
From sin and sorrow set us free,
And make thy temples worthy thee.

John Dryden (1631–1700)
English poet

Grant, almighty God, that as you shine on us by your Word, we may not be blind at midday, nor willfully seek darkness, and thus lull our minds asleep: but, may we be roused daily by your words, and may we stir up ourselves more and more to fear your name and thus present ourselves and all our pursuits, as a sacrifice to you, that you may peaceably rule and perpetually dwell in us, until you gather us to your celestial habitation, where there is reserved for us eternal rest and glory, through Jesus Christ our Lord. Amen.

John Calvin

Lord God, let us keep your Scriptures in mind and meditate on them day and night, persevering in prayer, always on the watch. We beg you, Lord, to give us real knowledge of what we read and to show us not only how to understand it, but how to put it into practice, so that we may deserve to obtain spiritual grace, enlightened by the law of the Holy Spirit, through Jesus Christ our Lord, whose power and glory will endure throughout all ages. Amen.

Origen of Alexandria (c.185–c.254)
First systematic theologian

Almighty God, our heavenly Father, without whose help labor is useless, without whose light search is vain, invigorate my studies and direct my enquiries, that I may by due diligence and right discernment establish myself and others in your holy faith. Take not, O Lord, your Holy Spirit from me, let not evil thoughts have dominion in my mind. Let me not linger in ignorance and doubt, but enlighten and support me, for the sake of Jesus Christ our Lord. Amen.

Samuel Johnson (1709–1784)
English writer and lexicographer

Take away, O Lord, the veil of my heart while I read the Scriptures. Blessed are you, O Lord: O teach me your statutes: give me a word, O Word of the Father: touch my heart: enlighten the understandings of my heart: open my lips and fill them with your praise: be, O Lord, in my spirit and in my mouth: in my mouth that lawfully and worthily I may show forth your oracles by the sanctifying power of your thrice Holy Spirit.

Lancelot Andrewes (1555–1626)
Bishop of Winchester and scholar

Blessed Lord, by whose providence all Holy Scriptures were written and preserved for our instruction: give us grace to study them each day with patience and love; strengthen our souls with the fullness of their divine teaching; keep us from all pride and irreverence; guide us in the deep things of your heavenly wisdom; and, of your great mercy, lead us by your Word into everlasting life.

Brooke Foss Westcott (1825–1901)
Bishop of Durham, biblical scholar

Almighty and most merciful God, you have given the Bible to be the revelation of your great love to us, and of your power and will to save us: grant that our study of it may not be made in vain by the callousness or carelessness of our hearts, but that by it we may be confirmed in penitence, lifted to hope, made strong for service, and, above all, filled with the true knowledge of yourself and of your Son Jesus Christ.

Sir George Adam Smith (1856–1942)
Biblical scholar and principal of the
University of Aberdeen

Almighty God, who created humanity after your image and gave them living souls that they may seek you and rule your creation, teach us so to investigate the works of your hand that we may subdue the earth to our use, and strengthen our intelligence for your service. And grant that we may so receive your Word as to believe in him whom you sent to give us the science of salvation and the forgiveness of our sins. All this we ask of you in the name of the same Jesus Christ our Lord. Amen.

James Clerk Maxwell (1831–1879)
Scottish physicist and inventor

O God, light of the minds that see you, life of the souls that love you, and strength of the souls that seek you, enlarge our minds and raise the vision of our hearts, that, with swift wings of thought, our spirits may reach you, the eternal wisdom, you who live from everlasting to everlasting; through Jesus Christ our Lord. Amen.

St. Augustine of Hippo (354–430)
First philosopher of Christianity, author of
The Confessions, *and theologian*

O Father! You who gave the visible light as the first-born of your creatures, and poured into human beings the intellectual light as the top and consummation of your workmanship, be pleased to protect and govern this work, which coming from your goodness returns to your glory. Then, after you had reviewed the works which your hands had made, you saw that "everything was very good"; and you rested with complacency in them. But humans, reflecting on the works which they had made, saw that "all was vanity and vexation of spirit," and could by no means acquiesce in them. Wherefore, if we labor in your works with the sweat of our brows, you will make us partakers of your vision and your sabbath. We humbly beg that this mind may be steadfastly in us, and that you, by our hands and also by the hands of others on whom you shall bestow the same Spirit, will please to convey a largeness of new alms to your family of mankind. These things we commend to your everlasting love, by our Jesus, your Christ, God with us. Amen.

Francis Bacon (1561–1626)
Lord chancellor of England and author

Dear Jesus,
Help us to spread your fragrance everywhere we go.
Flood our souls with your spirit and life.
Penetrate and possess our whole being so utterly
    that our lives may only be a radiance of yours. . . .
Let us thus praise you in the way you love best
    by shining on those around us.
Let us preach you without preaching
    not by words, but by our example
    by the catching force
    the sympathetic influence of what we do
    the evident fullness of the love our hearts bear to you.
                        Amen.

Mother Teresa of Calcutta (b. 1910)
Founder of the Sisters of Charity
    (prayer of the Missionaries of Charity,
    adapted from John Henry Newman)

8. To Know, Love, and Serve God

O God, you are the light of the minds that know you, the life of the souls that love you, and the strength of the wills that serve you; help us so to know you that we may truly love you, so to love you that we may fully serve you, whom to serve is perfect freedom; through Jesus Christ our Lord.

> *St. Augustine of Hippo (354–430)*
> *First philosopher of Christianity, author of*
> The Confessions, *and theologian*

O most merciful Redeemer, friend and brother, may we know you more clearly, love you more dearly, and follow you more nearly, for your own sake.

> *St. Richard of Chichester (c.1198–1253)*
> *English prelate*

Open wide the window of our spirits, O Lord, and fill us full of light; open wide the door of our hearts, that we may receive and entertain you with all our powers of adoration and love.

> *Christina Rossetti (1830–1894)*
> *English poet*

Give us a pure heart that we may see you,
A humble heart that we may hear you,
A heart of love that we may serve you,
A heart of faith that we may abide in you.

Dag Hammarskjöld (1905–1961)
Secretary-General of the United Nations

We love you, O our God; and we desire to love you more and more. Grant to us that we may love you as much as we desire, and as much as we ought. O dearest friend, who has so loved and saved us, the thought of whom is so sweet and always growing sweeter, come with Christ and dwell in our hearts; then you will keep a watch over our lips, our steps, our deeds, and we shall not need to be anxious either for our souls or our bodies. Give us love, sweetest of all gifts, which knows no enemy. Give us in our hearts pure love, born of your love to us, that we may love others as you love us. O most loving Father of Jesus Christ, from whom flows all love, let our hearts, frozen in sin, cold to you and cold to others, be warmed by this divine fire. So help and bless us in your Son. Amen.

St. Anselm (1033–1109)
Philosopher, archbishop of Canterbury

O God, Creator of all things, you are perpetually renewing the face of the world and have created us new in Jesus Christ; grant that in our worship of you and in communion with you, your created energy may more and more flood our lives, so that we may play our part in the fulfillment of your purpose, which transcends all that we can think or understand. Amen.

Willem Visser 't Hooft (1900–1985)
First secretary-general of the
World Council of Churches

See, Lord, an empty vessel that needs to be filled. My Lord, fill it. I am weak in the faith; strengthen me. I am cold in love; warm me and make me fervent so that my love may go out to my neighbor. I do not have a strong and firm faith; at times I doubt and am unable to trust you altogether. O Lord, help me. Strengthen my faith and trust in you. In you I have sealed all the treasures I have. I am poor; you are rich and came to be merciful to the poor. I am a sinner; you are upright. With me there is an abundance of sin; in you is the fullness of righteousness. Therefore, I will remain with you from whom I can receive, but to whom I may not give. Amen.

Martin Luther (1483–1546)
The great German reformer

Teach me thy love to know;
That this new light, which now I see,
May both the work and workman show:
Then by a sunne-beam I will climbe to thee.

George Herbert (1593–1633)
Anglican divine and metaphysical poet

O most tender and gentle Lord Jesus, teach me so to contemplate you that I may become like you and love you sincerely and simply as you have loved me.

John Henry Newman (1801–1890)
Cardinal, theologian, and man of letters

9. For Compassion and Service

Why should I live but to Thy praise?
  My life is hid with Thee.
O Lord, no longer be my days
  Than I may fruitful be.

> *Anne Bradstreet (1612–1672)*
> *New England poet and Puritan*

Lord, make me an instrument of your peace. Where there is hatred, let me sow love; where there is injury, pardon; where there is doubt, faith; where there is despair, hope; where there is darkness, light; where there is sadness, joy.

O divine Master, grant that I may not so much seek to be consoled, as to console; to be understood, as to understand; to be loved, as to love. For it is in giving that we receive; it is in pardoning that we are pardoned; and it is in dying that we are born to eternal life.

> *Attributed to St. Francis of Assisi*
> *(1181–1226)*
> *Founder of the Franciscan orders*

And give me, good Lord, a humble, lowly, quiet, peaceable, patient, charitable, kind and filial and tender mind, every shade, in fact, of charity; with all my words and all my works, and all my thoughts, to have a taste of your truly blessed Spirit.

> *Sir Thomas More (1478–1535)*
> *Lord chancellor of England and martyr*
> *(He wrote this prayer while imprisoned.)*

Grant us grace, O Father, not to pass by suffering or joy without eyes to see; give us understanding and sympathy; and guard us from selfishness that we may enter into the joys and sufferings of others; use us to gladden and strengthen those who are weak and suffering; that by our lives we may help others who believe and serve you, and project your light which is the light of life.

H. R. L. Sheppard (1880–1937)
Vicar of St. Martin-in-the-Fields, London

Dearest Lord, may I see you today and every day in the person of your sick, and whils't nursing them minister to you.

Though you hide yourself behind the unattractive disguise of the irritable, the exacting, the unreasonable, may I still recognize you and say "Jesu, my patient, how sweet it is to serve you."

Lord, give me this seeing faith, then my work will never be monotonous. I will ever find joy in humoring the fancies and gratifying the wishes of all poor sufferers.

O beloved sick, how doubly dear you are to me, when you personify Christ; and what a privilege is mine to be allowed to tend you.

Sweetest Lord, make me appreciative of the dignity of my high vocation and its many responsibilities. Never permit me to disgrace it by giving way to coldness, unkindness or impatience.

And, O God, while you are Jesus my patient, deign also to be to me a patient Jesus, bearing with my faults, looking only to my intention, which is to love and serve you in the person of each of your sick.

Lord, increase my faith, bless my effort and work, now and for evermore.

Daily prayer of Mother Teresa of Calcutta
(b. 1910)
Founder of the Sisters of Charity

Make us worthy, Lord,
To serve our fellow-men
Throughout the world who live and die
In poverty or hunger.

Give them through our hands
This day their daily bread
And by our understanding love
Give peace and joy.

Mother Teresa of Calcutta

You are never weary, O Lord, of doing us good. Let us never be weary of serving you. But as you have pleasure in the prosperity of your servants, so let us take pleasure in the service of our Lord, and abound in your work, and in your love and praise evermore. O fill up all that is wanting, reform whatever is amiss in us, perfect what concerns us, let the witness of our pardoning love ever abide in all our hearts.

John Wesley (1703–1791)
Anglican priest and founder of the
Methodist Church

O Lord, our Savior, you have warned us that you will require much of those to whom much is given; grant that we whose lot is cast in so godly a heritage may strive together the more abundantly to extend to others what we so richly enjoy; and as we have entered into the labors of others, so to labor that others may enter into ours, to the fulfillment of your holy will; through Jesus Christ our Lord.

St. Augustine of Hippo (354–430)
First philosopher of Christianity, author of
The Confessions, *and theologian*

10. For Courage

Teach us, good Lord, to serve you as you deserve:
To give and not to count the cost;
To fight and not to heed the wounds;
To toil and not to seek for rest;
To labor and not to ask for any reward
Save that of knowing that we do your will.

> *St. Ignatius of Loyola (1491–1556)*
> *Founder of the Society of Jesus and author*
> *of the* Spiritual Exercises

O God, you gave us the grace to carry the sword of your kingdom of peace; and you made us messengers of peace in a world of strife, and messengers of strife in a world of false peace: make strong our hand, make clear our voice, give us humility with firmness and insight with passion, that we may fight not to conquer but to redeem.

> *Gregory Vlastos (b. 1907)*
> *Professor of philosophy, Princeton University*

O Prince of Life, teach us to stand more boldly on your side, to face the world and all our adversaries more courageously, and not to let ourselves be dismayed by any storm of temptation; may our eyes be steadfastly fixed on you in fearless faith; may we trust you with perfect confidence that you will keep us, save us, and bring us through by the power of your grace and the riches of your mercy.

> *Gerhard Tersteegen (1697–1769)*
> *German Protestant devotional writer*
> *and mystic*

O Lord Christ, who, when your hour was come, went without fear amongst those who sought your life: grant us grace to confess you before all, without arrogance and without fear, that your Holy Name may be glorified.

J. H. Oldham (1874–1969)
Missionary statesman and leader of the
ecumenical movement

O heavenly Father, the Father of all wisdom, understanding and true strength, I beg you, look mercifully on me and send your Holy Spirit into my breast; that when I must join to fight in the field for the glory of your Holy Name, then I, being strengthened with the defense of your right hand, may manfully stand in the confession of your faith and of your truth, and continue in the same to the end of my life, through our Lord Jesus Christ. Amen.

Nicholas Ridley (c.1503–1555)
Bishop of London and Marian martyr

Much remains
To conquer still; peace hath her victories
No less renowned than war; new foes arise,
Threatening to bind our souls with secular chains.
Help us to save free conscience from the paw
Of hireling wolves, whose gospel is their maw.

John Milton (1608–1674)
English poet

11. For Joy and Contentment

Dig out of us, O Lord, the venomous roots of covetousness; or else so repress them with your grace, that we may be contented with your provision of necessaries, and not labor, as we do, with all toil, sleight, guile, wrong and oppression, to pamper ourselves with vain superfluities.

> *Edmund Grindal (c.1519–1583)*
> *Bishop of London, archbishop*
> *of Canterbury*

Pale care, avaunt!
I'll learn to be content
With that small stock your bounty gave or lent.
What may conduce
To my most healthful use,
Almighty God, me grant;
But that, or this,
That hurtful is
Deny your suppliant.

> *Robert Herrick (1591–1674)*
> *Anglican priest and poet*

O Lord, keep us sensitive to the grace that is around us. May the familiar not become neglected. May we see your goodness in our daily bread, and may the comforts of our home take our thoughts to the mercifulness of God; through Jesus Christ. Amen.

J. H. Jowett (1864–1923)
Minister of Fifth Avenue Presbyterian
Church, New York City, and of
Westminster Chapel, London

Come and help us, Lord Jesus. A vision of your face will brighten us; but to feel your Spirit touching us will make us vigorous. Oh! for the leaping and walking of the man born lame. May we today dance with holy joy, like David before the ark of God. May a holy exhilaration take possession of every part of us; may we be glad in the Lord; may our mouth be filled with laughter, and our tongue with singing, "for the Lord hath done great things for us whereof we are glad."

Charles H. Spurgeon (1834–1892)
English Baptist minister and
biblical expositor

O God, as the day returns and brings us the petty round of irritating duties, help us to perform them with laughter and kind faces; let cheerfulness abound with industry; give us to go blithely on our business all this day; bring us to our resting beds weary and content and undishonored; and grant us in the end the gift of sleep.

Robert Louis Stevenson (1850–1894)
Scottish essayist, novelist, and poet

Help us, O God, to look back on the long way you have brought us, on the long days in which we have been served, not according to our deserts, but our desires; on the pit and the miry clay, the blackness of despair, the horror of misconduct, from which our feet have been plucked out. For our sins forgiven or prevented, for our shame unpublished, we bless and thank you, O God. Help us yet again and ever. So order events, so strengthen our frailty, as that day by day we shall come before you with this song of gratitude, and in the end be dismissed with honor. In their weakness and in their fear, the vessels of your handiwork so pray to you, so praise to you. Amen.

Robert Louis Stevenson

Almighty God, give us a measure of true religion and thereby set us free from vain and disappointing hopes, from lawless and exorbitant appetites, from frothy and empty joys, from anxious, self-devouring cares, from a dull and black melancholy, from an eating envy and swelling pride, and from rigid sourness and severity of spirit, so that we may possess that peace which passeth all understanding, through Jesus Christ our Lord.

Benjamin Whichcote (1609–1683)
English philosopher, Cambridge Platonist

O Christ, you were called the man of sorrows, and yet you prayed for your disciples that they might have your joy; grant us such sympathy as takes upon itself the burden of the sorrowing; and with it such glad courage as shall turn the way of sadness into the way of joy, because we follow in your footsteps, O blessed Master, Jesus Christ. Amen.

Walter Russell Bowie (1882–1969)
Rector of Grace Episcopal Church,
New York City

12. For Amendment and Growth in Grace

Batter my heart, three person'd God; for you
As yet but knock, breathe, shine, and seek to mend;
That I may rise, and stand, o'erthrow me, and bend
Your force to break, blow, burn, and make me new.

John Donne (1572–1631)
Metaphysical poet and dean of
St. Paul's Cathedral, London

O blessed Jesus, you know the impurity of our affection, the narrowness of our sympathy, and the coldness of our love; take possession of our souls and fill our minds with the image of yourself; break the stubbornness of our selfish wills and mold us in the likeness of your unchanging love, O you who alone can do this, our Savior, our Lord and our God.

William Temple (1881–1944)
Archbishop of Canterbury and president of
the Workers' Educational Association

Grant, O our God, that we may know you, love you and rejoice in you; and if in this life we cannot do these things fully, grant that we may at the least progress in them from day to day, for Christ's sake. Amen.

St. Anselm (1033–1109)
Philosopher, archbishop of Canterbury

O Jesus Christ, the mirror of all gentleness of mind, the example of highest obedience and patience, grant us your servants with true devotion to consider how you, innocent and undefiled Lamb, were bound, taken, and hailed away to death for our sins; how well content you were to suffer such things, not opening your mouth in impatience, but willingly offering yourself unto death. O gracious God, how vilely were you mishandled for our sakes! O Lord, let this never come out of our hearts. Expel through it coldness and sloth; stir up love and fervency towards you; provoke us to earnest prayer and make us cheerful and diligent in your will. . . . Amen.

Miles Coverdale (c.1488–1569)
English reformer and translator of the Bible

Grant, I beg you, merciful Lord, that the designs of a new and better life, which by your grace I have now formed, may not pass away without effect. Incite and enable me, by your Holy Spirit, to improve the time which you shall grant me; to avoid all evil thoughts, words, and actions; and to do all the duties which you shall set before me. Hear my prayer, O Lord, for the sake of Jesus Christ.

Samuel Johnson (1702–1784)
English writer and lexicographer

O God, who by love alone are great and glorious, you are present and live with us by love alone: grant us likewise by love to attain another self, by love to live in others, and by love to come to our glory, to see and accompany your love throughout eternity.

Thomas Traherne (1636–1674)
English poet and minister of the
Church of Wales

O God, take all our sorrows and use them to show us the nature of your joy. Take all our sins and, forgiving them, use them to show us the ways of true pleasantness and the path of true peace. Take all our broken purposes and disappointed hopes and use them to make your perfect rainbow arch. Take all our clouds of sadness and calamity and from them make your sunset glories. Take our night and make it bright with stars. Take our ill-health and pain until they accomplish in your purpose as much as health could achieve. Take us as we are with impulses, strivings, longings so often frustrated and thwarted, and even with what is broken and imperfect, make your dreams come true, through him who made of human life a sacrament, of thorns a crown, of a cross a throne, even through Jesus Christ our Lord.

Leslie D. Weatherhead (1893–1976)
Minister of the City Temple, London

Lord Jesus, all power is given to you in heaven and earth: transform our understandings and our wills; cleanse our hearts; send your Holy Spirit into our souls; subdue us to yourself, so that our flesh may be brought into subjection to the Spirit, and our affections made obedient to your pure and holy law, to the praise and glory of your sovereign grace.

Juan Luis Vives (1492–1540)
Spanish educator and humanist

We must praise your goodness that you have left nothing undone to draw us to yourself. But one thing we ask of you, our God, not to cease to work in our improvement. Let us tend towards you, no matter by what means, and be fruitful in good works, for the sake of Jesus Christ our Lord.

Ludwig van Beethoven (1770–1827)
German composer

O Lord, reassure me with your quickening Spirit; without you I can do nothing. Mortify in me all ambition, vanity, vainglory, worldliness, pride, selfishness, and resistance from God, and fill me with love, peace, and all the fruits of the Spirit. O Lord, I know not what I am, but to you I flee for refuge. I would surrender myself to you, trusting your precious promises and against hope believing in hope. You are the same yesterday, today, and for ever; and therefore, waiting on the Lord, I trust I shall at length renew my strength.

William Wilberforce (1759–1833)
English evangelical abolitionist

Lord, make me see your glory in every place:
   If mortal beauty sets my heart aglow,
   Shall not that earthly fire by yours burn low
Extinguished by the great light of your grace?

Dear Lord, I cry to you for help, O raise
   Me from the misery of this blind woe,
   Your spirit alone can save me: let it flow
Through will and sense, redeeming what is base.

You have given me on earth this god-like soul,
And a poor prisoner of it you have made
Behind weak flesh-woes: from that wretched state

How can I rescue it, how my true life find?
All goodness, Lord, must fail without your aid:
For you alone have power to alter fate.

Michelangelo Buonarroti (1475–1564)
Italian painter, sculptor, architect, and poet

13. For the Full Use of One's Talents for God

O lead my spirit, O raise it from these weary depths, that ravished
by your Art, it may strive upwards with tempestuous fire. For you
alone have knowledge, you alone can inspire enthusiasm.

Ludwig van Beethoven (1770–1827)
German composer

God give me work
Till my life shall end
And life
Till my work is done.

Winifred Holtby (1898–1935)
English novelist

Almighty God, the giver of wisdom, without whose help resolutions are vain, without whose blessing study is ineffectual; enable me, if it be your will, to attain such knowledge as may qualify me to direct the doubtful, and instruct the ignorant; to prevent wrongs and terminate contentions; and grant that I may use that knowledge which I shall attain to your glory and my own salvation, for Jesus Christ's sake.

Samuel Johnson (1709–1784)
English writer and lexicographer

Teach me, my God and King,
    In all things thee to see,
And what I do in anything,
    To do it as for thee!
All may of thee partake,
    Nothing can be so mean,
Which with this tincture (for thy sake)
    Will not grow bright and clean.
A servant with this clause
    Makes drudgery divine!
Who sweeps a room as for thy laws
    Makes that and th'action fine.

George Herbert (1593–1633)
Anglican divine and metaphysical poet

Lord, slay sloth within us and never let us find a pillow for doctrines of grace for ease while yet a single sin remains. . . . O keep us, we beg you, Lord, for without your keeping, we cannot keep ourselves.

Charles H. Spurgeon (1834–1892)
English Baptist minister and
biblical expositor

Grant us grace, our Father, to do our work this day as workers who need not be ashamed. Give us the spirit of diligence and honest enquiry in our quest for the spirit of charity in all our dealings with our fellows, and the spirit of gaiety, courage, and a quiet mind in facing all tasks and responsibilities.

Reinhold Niebuhr (1892–1971)
Professor of Applied Christian Ethics,
Union Theological Seminary, New York

Eternal and most glorious God, you have stamped the soul of humanity with your Image, received it into your revenue, and made it part of your treasure; do not allow us so to undervalue ourselves, so to impoverish you, as to give away these souls for nothing, and all the world is nothing if the soul must be given for it. Do this, O God, for his sake who knows our natural infirmities, for he had them, and knows the weight of our sins, for he paid a dear price for them; your Son, our Savior Jesus Christ.

John Donne (1572–1631)
Metaphysical poet and dean of
St. Paul's Cathedral, London

PRAYERS OF PETITION

14. For Humility

Grant, almighty God, as no other way of access to you is open for us except through unfeigned humility, that we often learn to abase ourselves with feelings of true repentance. May we be so displeased with ourselves as not to be satisfied with a single confession of our iniquities. May we continue to meditate on our sins until we are more and more penetrated with real grief. Then may we fly to your mercy, prostrate ourselves before you in silence and acknowledge no other hope than your pity, and the intercession of your only-begotten Son. May we be reconciled to you, absolved from our sins, and governed throughout the whole course of our life by your Holy Spirit. Let us at length enjoy the victory in every kind of contest, and arrive at that blessed rest which you have prepared for us by the same, our Lord Jesus Christ. Amen.

John Calvin (1509–1564)
French theologian and reformer in Geneva

O God, grant that looking upon the face of the Lord as into a glass, we may be changed into his likeness, from glory to glory. Take out of us all pride and vanity, boasting and forwardness, and give us the true courage which shows itself by gentleness, the true wisdom which shows itself by simplicity, and the true power which shows itself by modesty.

Charles Kingsley (1819–1875)
Anglican clergyman, novelist, and
Christian socialist

God in heaven,
Let me really feel my nothingness,
Not in order to despair over it,
But in order to feel the more powerfully
The greatness of your goodness.

Søren Kierkegaard (1813–1855)
Danish philosopher and theologian

O Lord, teach us to humble ourselves before these children who live the Gospel of love and drugs because we did not live the Gospel of love. Teach us to humble ourselves before the problems that face our children in this generation. Especially we pray for all parents, that they may love their children steadfastly, even in the face of bewilderment and grief. Teach us to humble ourselves when we contemplate the world we have made, the millions that we have killed and maimed in the course of justice. And above all make us instruments of your love, that we may love those who call out that they love us all. Even if we cannot help them, teach us to love them.

All this we ask in the name of God, who so loved the world, and of his son Jesus, the lover of our souls.

Alan Paton (1903–1989)
South African novelist

O everliving God, let this mind be in us which was also in Christ Jesus; that as he from his loftiness stooped to the death of the Cross; so we in our loneliness may humble ourselves, believing, obeying, living, and dying to the glory of the Father; for the same Jesus Christ's sake.

Christina Rossetti (1830–1894)
English poet

O Lord, who has taught us that to gain the whole world and to lose our souls is great folly, grant us grace so to lose ourselves that we may truly find ourselves anew in the life of grace, and so to forget ourselves that we may be remembered in your kingdom.

Reinhold Niebuhr (1892–1971)
Professor of Applied Christian Ethics,
Union Theological Seminary, New York

15. For Peace and Serenity

Serene Son of God, whose will subdued the troubled waters and led to rest the fears of the people: let your majesty master us, your power of calm control us; that for our fears we have faith, and for our disquietude perfect trust in you; who live and govern all things, world without end.

John Wallace Suter (1890–1977)
Dean of Washington Cathedral

So teach us to number our days that we may apply our hearts to wisdom. Lighten, if it be your will, the pressure of this world's care, and, above all, reconcile us to your will, and give us a peace which the world cannot take away; through Jesus Christ our Lord. Amen.

Thomas Chalmers (1780–1847)
Scottish theologian and preacher

Grant us, O Lord, the blessing of those whose minds are stayed on you, so that we may be kept in perfect peace: a peace which cannot be broken. Let not our minds rest upon any creature, but only in the Creator; not upon goods, things, houses, lands, inventions of vanities or foolish fashions, lest, our peace being broken, we become cross and brittle and given over to envy. From all such deliver us, O God, and grant us your peace.

George Fox (1624–1691)
Founder of the Society of Friends

God of all grace, give us your peace that passes understanding, that the quietness that comes from friendliness with human beings, and true divine friendship with you may possess our soul; that we, withdrawn awhile from the turmoil of the world, may gather the strength that we have lost, and established and strengthened by your grace, pass on through all the troubles of this our earthly life, safe into the haven of eternal rest; through Jesus Christ our Lord. Amen.

George Dawson (1821–1876)
English Baptist minister and founder of the
Church of our Saviour, Birmingham

O Lord, calm the waves of this heart; calm its tempests. Calm yourself, O my soul, so that the divine can act in you. Calm yourself, O my soul, so that God is able to repose in you, so that his peace may cover you. Yes, Father in heaven, often have we found that the world cannot give us peace, O but make us feel that you are able to give peace; let us know the truth of your promise: that the whole world may not be able to take away your peace.

Søren Kierkegaard (1813–1855)
Danish philosopher and theologian

Let us not seek out of you what we can
   only find in you, O Lord.
Peace and rest, and joy and bliss,
   which abide only in your abiding joy.
Lift up our souls above the weary round of
   harassing thoughts to your eternal presence.
Lift up our minds to the pure, bright, serene
   atmosphere of your presence,
      that we may breathe freely,
      there repose in your love,
      there be at rest from ourselves
      and from all things that weary us:
and thence return, arrayed in your peace,
      to do and to bear
   whatsoever shall best please you,
      O blessed Lord.

Edward Bouverie Pusey (1800–1882)
Canon of Christ Church and regius
   professor of Hebrew, Oxford University

16. For Forgiveness and Generosity of Spirit

Jesus, I wish you would let me wash your feet, since it was through walking about in me that you soiled them. I wish you would give me the task of wiping the stains from your feet, because it was my behavior that put them there. But where can I get the running water I need to wash your feet? If I have no water, at least I have my tears: let me wash your feet with them, and wash myself at the same time.

St. Ambrose (339–397)
Bishop of Milan

O Lord Jesus, because, being full of foolishness, we often sin and have to ask pardon, help us to forgive as we would be forgiven, neither mentioning old offenses committed against us, nor dwelling upon them in thought, nor being influenced by them in heart; but loving each other freely, as you freely love us; for your name's sake. Amen.

Christina Rossetti (1830–1894)
English poet

O Lord, give us more charity, more self-denial, more likeness to you. Teach us to sacrifice our comforts to others, and our likings for the sake of doing good. Make us kindly in thought, gentle in word, generous in deed. Teach us that it is better to give than to receive; better to forget ourselves than put ourselves forward; better to minister than be ministered to. And to you, the God of love, be glory and praise for ever. Amen.

Henry Alford (1810–1871)
Dean of Canterbury Cathedral

We come to you in penitence, confessing our sins: the vows we have forgotten, the opportunities we have let slip, the excuses whereby we have sought to deceive ourselves and you. Forgive us that we talk so much and are silent so seldom; that we are in such constant motion and are so rarely still; that we depend so implicitly on the effectiveness of our organizations and so little on the power of your Spirit. Teach us to wait upon you, that we may renew our strength, mount up with wings as eagles, run and not be weary, walk and not faint.

William Sloane Coffin, Jr. (b. 1924)
Minister of Riverside Church, New York City

17. For Patience and Perseverance

O Lord God, when you give to your servants to endeavor any great matter, grant us also to know that it is not the beginning, but the continuing of the same until it be thoroughly finished which yields the true glory.

Sir Francis Drake (1540–1596)
English privateer

O Lord, who call your own sheep by name, grant, we beg you, that all whom you call by the voice of conscience may straightway arise to do your most compassionate will, or abide patiently to suffer it. Amen.

Christina Rossetti (1830–1894)
English poet

O merciful God, be unto me a strong tower of defense; give me grace to await your leisure and patiently to bear what you are doing to me; nothing doubting or mistrusting your goodness towards me; for you know what is good for me better than I do. Therefore do with me in all things what you will; only arm me, I beseech you, with your armor, that I may stand fast; above all things, taking to me the shield of faith; praying always that I may refer myself wholly to your will, abiding your pleasure and comforting myself in these troubles which it shall please you to send me, seeing such troubles are profitable for me; and I am assuredly persuaded that all you do cannot but be well; and unto you be all honor and glory; Amen.

Lady Jane Grey (1537–1554)
Great-granddaughter of Henry VII charged
with treason and beheaded

18. For the Life Everlasting

Bring us, O Lord God, at our last awakening into the house and gate of heaven, to enter into that gate and dwell in that house, where there shall be no darkness nor dazzling, but one equal light; no noise nor silence, but one equal music; no fears nor hopes, but one equal possession; no ends nor beginnings, but one equal eternity; in the habitations of your glory and dominion, world without end.

John Donne (1572–1631)
Metaphysical poet and dean of
St. Paul's Cathedral, London

Grant, almighty God, since we have already entered in hope upon the threshold of our eternal inheritance, and know that there is a mansion for us in heaven since Christ, our head and the first fruits of our salvation, has been received there; grant that we may proceed more and more in the way of your holy calling until at length we reach the goal and so enjoy the eternal glory of which you have given us a taste in this world, by the same Christ our Lord.

John Calvin (1509–1564)
French theologian and reformer in Geneva

O God, you who have prepared a place for my soul, prepare my soul for that place; prepare it with holiness; prepare it with desire; and even while it remains on earth, let it dwell in heaven with you; seeing the beauty of your face and the glory of your saints, now and for evermore.

Joseph Hall (1574–1656)
Bishop of Norwich and epigrammatist

Almighty Father, Son, and Holy Ghost, eternal ever-blessed gracious God; to me the least of saints, to me allow that I may keep a door in paradise. That I may keep even the smallest door, the furthest, the darkest, coldest door, the door that is least used, the stiffest door. If so it be but in your house, O God, if it so be that I can see your glory even afar, and hear your voice, O God, and know that I am with you, O God.

> St. Columba of Iona (c.521–597)
> Irish missionary

Jesus whom I look at shrouded here below,
I beseech you send me what I thirst for so,
Some day to gaze on you face to face in light
And be blest for ever with your glory's sight.

> Latin, 13th century
> Translated by Gerard Manley Hopkins
> (1844–1889) English poet

O Lord our God, from whom neither life nor death can separate those who trust in your love, and whose love holds in its embrace your children in this world and in the next: so unite us to yourself that in fellowship with you we may be always united to our loved ones whether here or there; give us courage, constancy and hope; through him who died and was buried and rose again for us, Jesus Christ our Lord.

> William Temple (1881–1944)
> Archbishop of Canterbury and president of
> the Workers' Educational Association

O God, before whose face the generations rise and pass away, the strength of those who labor and suffer, and the repose of the holy and blessed dead, we rejoice in the communion of your saints. We remember all who have faithfully lived; all who have peacefully died, and especially those most dear to us. Lift us into light and love; give us at last our portion with those who have trusted in you and striven in all things to do your holy will. And to your name, with the Church on earth and the Church in heaven, we would ascribe all honor and glory, world without end. Amen.

John Hunter (1849–1917)
Minister of the King's Weigh House, London

We give back to you, O God, those whom you gave to us. You did not lose them when you gave them to us, and we do not lose them by their return to you. Your dear Son has taught us that life is eternal and love cannot die. So death is only an horizon and an horizon is only the limit of our sight. Open our eyes to see more clearly, and draw us closer to you that we may know that we are nearer to our loved ones who are with you. You have told us that you are preparing a place for us, prepare us also for that happy place, that where you are we may also be always, O dear Lord of life and death.

William Penn (1644–1718)
Quaker leader and founder of
Pennsylvania

O God, the God of the spirits of all flesh, in whose embrace all creatures live, in whatsoever world or condition they be; I beg you for him whose name and dwelling place and every need you know. Lord, grant him light and rest, peace, refreshment, joy, and consolation, in paradise, in the companionship of saints, in the presence of Christ, in the ample folds of your great love.

If in anything I can minister to his peace, be pleased of your love to let this be; and mercifully keep me from every act which may deprive me of the sight of him as soon as our trial time is over; or mar the fullness of our joy when the end of days shall come; through Jesus Christ our Lord. Amen.

William Ewart Gladstone (1809–1898)
English prime minister

19. For a Disciplined Life

Grant, almighty God, that as we do not at this day look for a redeemer to deliver us from temporal miseries, but only carry on a warfare under the banner of the Cross until he appear to us from heaven to gather us into his blessed kingdom—O grant that we may patiently bear all evils and all troubles, and as Christ once for all poured forth the blood of the new and eternal covenant, and gave us also a symbol of it in the Holy Supper, may we, confiding in so sacred a seal, never doubt that he will always be propitious to us, and render manifest to us the fruit of this reconciliation, when, after having supported us for a season under the burden of those miseries by which we are now oppressed, you gather us into that blessed and perfect glory which has been procured for us by the blood of Christ our Lord, and which is daily set before us in his Gospel, and laid up for us in heaven, until we at length shall enjoy it through Christ our only Lord. Amen.

John Calvin (1509–1564)
French theologian and reformer in Geneva

May Jesus Christ, the King of glory, help us to make the right use of all the suffering that comes to us and to offer to him the incense of a patient and trustful heart; for his name's sake. Amen.

Johannes Tauler (c.1300–1361)
German mystic and preacher

O God, by our great Master's example you have taught us what labors and sufferings heaven deserves, and that we are to take it by force; confound in us, we beg you, the nice tenderness of our nature, which is averse to that discipline and hardship we ought to endure as disciples and soldiers of Jesus Christ; help us in our way thither, by self-denial and mortification, for the sake of our Lord Jesus Christ, who lives and reigns with you and your Holy Spirit, ever one God, world without end.

John Wesley (1703–1791)
Anglican priest and founder of the
Methodist Church

O Jesus, poor and abject, unknown and despised, have mercy upon me and let me not be ashamed to follow you.

O Jesus, hated, calumniated, and persecuted, have mercy upon me, and let me not be afraid to come after you.

O Jesus, betrayed and sold at a vile price, have mercy upon me and make me content to be as my Master.

O Jesus, blasphemed, accused, and wrongfully condemned, have mercy upon me and teach me to endure the contradiction of sinners.

O Jesus, clothed with a habit of reproach and shame, have mercy upon me, and let me not seek my own glory.

O Jesus, insulted, mocked, and spit upon, have mercy upon me and let me run with patience the race set before me.

O Jesus, dragged to the pillar, scourged and bathed in blood, have mercy upon me, and let me not faint in the fiery trial.

O Jesus, crowned with thorns and hailed in derision;

O Jesus, burdened with our sins and the curses of the people;

O Jesus, affronted, outraged, buffeted, overwhelmed with injuries, griefs, and humiliations;

O Jesus, hanging on the accursed Tree, bowing the head, giving up the ghost, have mercy upon me, and conform my whole soul to your holy, humble, suffering Spirit.

John Wesley

Grant to us, O Father, the wisdom that is necessary in all the conduct of life. And grant that even our mistakes may rise up to guide us and when we behold the mistakes of others, while we seek to rescue them and to sympathize with them, grant that we may read likewise the lessons which they make for us.

Henry Ward Beecher (1813–1887)
American Congregational minister
and social reformer

I said, "Let me walk in the fields."
  He said, "Nay, walk in the town."
I said, "There are no flowers there."
  He said, "No flowers, but a crown."

I said, "But the sky is black,
  There is nothing but noise and din."
But he wept as he sent me back—
  "There is more," he said, "there is sin."

George MacDonald (1824–1905)
Scottish novelist and Christian apologist

Help me, O Lord, to make a true use of all disappointments and calamities in this life, in such a way that they may unite my heart more closely with you. Cause them to separate my affections from worldly things and inspire my soul with more vigor in the pursuit of true happiness.

Susanna Wesley (1669–1742)
Mother of 19 children, including
John and Charles Wesley, and author

Lord, give me patience in tribulation and grace in everything to conform my will to you, that I may truly say: "Your will be done, on earth as it is in heaven."

The things, good Lord, that I pray for, give me your grace to labor for.

Sir Thomas More (1478–1535)
Lord chancellor of England and martyr

I did not know you, my Lord, because I still desired to know and delight in things.

Well and good if all things change, Lord God, provided we are rooted in you.

If I go everywhere with you, my God, everywhere things will happen as I desire for your sake.

St. John of the Cross (1542–1591)
Carmelite mystic and poet

O God, let the plowshare of your stern mercy break the complacent ground of our souls; let the broad hand of your providence strew the soil with the seed of circumstance; and in your time, grant us a harvest of hours and life in which the labor and suffering of our hearts shall be fruitful with eternal grain.

Samuel H. Miller (1900–1968)
Dean of Harvard Divinity School
and Baptist minister

Gracious Father, be pleased to touch our hearts in time with trouble, with sorrow, with sickness, with disappointment, with anything that may hinder them from being hard to the end, and leading us to eternal ruin.

Thomas Arnold (1795–1842)
Headmaster of Rugby School and father of
Matthew Arnold

20. To Overcome Racial and Class Prejudices

I see white and black, Lord.
I see white teeth in a black face.
I see black eyes in a white face.
Help us to see *persons*, Jesus—not a black person or a white person,
a red person or a yellow person, but human persons.

Malcolm Boyd (b. 1923)
American Episcopal priest

Holy be the white head of a negro,
Sacred be the black flax of a black child.
Holy be the golden down
That will stream in the waves of the wind
And will thin like dispersing cloud.
Holy be the heads of Chinese hair,
Sea calm, sea impersonal
Deep flowering of the mellow and traditional.
Heads of peoples fair
Bright shimmering from the riches of their species:
Heads of Indians
With feeling of distance and space and dusk:
Heads of wheaten gold,
Heads of peoples dark
So strong, so original,
All of the earth and the sun.

George Campbell (b. 1916)
Contemporary Jamaican poet

O Lord Christ, who came that we might have life and have it more abundantly, so come that all shall have full opportunity to live; so come that we may open out opportunities to all who are dear to you because they lack and suffer hunger. Come and break down all that hinders life, the iron walls of grim refusal that give life no chance. Come and give us wisdom and patience, courage and resolution to discover how your goodwill may verify itself to all. Give us life that we may give out life. Come and fill us with your own strong desire; with your own brave hope, that all may find their way to live in you. Give unity; give brotherhood; give peace.

H. Scott Holland (1847–1918)
Theologian and canon of St. Paul's
Cathedral, London

O Lord Jesus Christ, in whom all differences of class are done away, take from us all pride, envy, and prejudice. Unite us one to another by a common zeal for your cause, and enable us by your grace to offer to you the manifold fruits of our service.

Brooke Foss Westcott (1825–1901)
Bishop of Durham, biblical scholar

O God, the king of righteousness, lead us, we pray you, in the ways of justice and of peace; inspire us to break down all oppression and wrong, to gain for everyone their due reward, and from everyone their due service; that each may live for all and all may care for each, in the name of Jesus Christ our Lord.

William Temple (1881–1944)
Archbishop of Canterbury and president of
the Workers' Educational Association

21. For Benefits from Receiving the Sacraments

God, the all-powerful, Father of Christ, who is your only Son, give me a clean body, a pure heart, a watchful mind and knowledge free from error. May your Holy Spirit come to me and bring me truth, yes, and the fullness of truth through your Christ. Through him may glory be yours, in the Holy Spirit, throughout the ages. Amen.

The Apostolic Constitutions

May this your sacrament, Lord Jesus Christ,
bring life to us and pardon for our sins,
to us for whom you suffered your passion.

For our sake you drank gall
to kill in us the bitterness
that is the Enemy's.

For our sake you drank sour wine
to strengthen what is weak in us.

For our sake you were spat upon
to bathe us in the dew of immortality.

You were struck with a frail reed
to strengthen what is frail in us
and give us life for all eternity.

You were crowned with thorns
to crown those who believe in you
with that ever-green garland, your charity.

You were wrapped in a shroud
to clothe us in your all-enfolding strength.

You were laid in a new grave
to give us new grace in ages likewise new.

The Apocryphal Acts of Thomas, 3rd century

Grant, O Lord, that as we leave your house, we may not leave your presence, but walk in your paths all the days of our life, through Jesus Christ our Lord.

Edward Lambe Parsons (1888–1960)
Bishop of the Episcopal Church, California

PART 4

PRAYERS OF INTERCESSION

1. For the Church

Most gracious Father, we humbly beg you for your Holy Catholic Church; that you would be pleased to fill it with all truth, in all peace. Where it is corrupt, purify it; where it is in error, direct it; where in any thing it is amiss, reform it. Where it is right, strengthen and confirm it; where it is in want, provide for it; where it is divided and rent asunder, do make up the breaches in it, O holy one of Israel.

William Laud (1573–1645)
Archbishop of Canterbury

O God our Creator, we pray for your Church, and specifically for this church: may it be free, courageous, and compassionate, not fearful or rigid; a safe harbor when the winds of the world are high against us, and the only safe ship in which to sail out of the harbor to take on the storms of life. . . . O Jesus Christ, bleeding and broken and bowed, yet still unconquered, you who reign from the Cross, pour out your Spirit on all your Churches. Revive your work. Raise up laborers, O Lord, that men and women may be ready to tell of your justice and peace and of your salvation until the ends of the earth. Amen.

William Sloane Coffin, Jr. (b. 1924)
Minister of Riverside Church, New York City

O God, we pray for your Church, which is set today amid the perplexities of a changing order, and face to face with a great new task. We remember with love the nurture she gave to our spiritual life in its infancy, the tasks she set for our growing strength, the influence of the devoted hearts she gathers, the steadfast power for good she has exerted. When we compare her with all human institutions, we rejoice, for there is none like her. But when we judge her by the mind of the Master, we bow in pity and contrition. Oh, baptize her afresh in the life-giving spirit of Jesus! Grant her a new birth, though it be with the travail of repentance and humiliation. Bestow upon her a more imperious responsiveness to duty, a swifter compassion with suffering, and an utter loyalty to the will of God. Put upon her lips the ancient Gospel of her Lord. Help her to proclaim boldly the coming of the kingdom of God and the doom of all that resist it. Fill her with the prophets' scorn of tyranny, and with a Christ-like tenderness for the heavy-laden and down-trodden. Give her faith to espouse the cause of the people, and in their hands that grope after freedom and light to recognize the bleeding hands of Christ. Bid her cease from seeking her own life, lest she lose it. Make her valiant to give up her life to humanity, that like her crucified Lord, she may mount by the path of the Cross to a higher glory.

Walter Rauschenbusch (1861–1918)
American Baptist minister and exponent of
the Social Gospel

God, our Shepherd, give to the Church a new vision and a new charity, new wisdom and fresh understanding, the revival of her brightness and the renewal of her unity; that the eternal message of your Son, undefiled by human tradition, may be hailed as the good news of the new age; through him who makes all things new, Jesus Christ our Lord.

Percy Dearmer (1867–1936)
Anglican priest, historian, and hymnologist

O Lord of changeless power and endless life, be favorable to your Church throughout the world. Gather, enlighten, sanctify and sustain it by your Holy Spirit. Give us more and more to trust the silent working of your perpetual grace, which brings forth in Christ the salvation of humanity. And let the whole world know that the things which were cast down are being raised up, and the things which had grown old are being made new, and all the things are returning to the perfection of him from whom they came. Amen.

Peter Taylor Forsyth (1848–1921)
Congregational minister and theologian

O God, we do not desire new contentions and discord. We pray only that the Son of God, our Lord Jesus Christ, who for us died and rose from the grave, will guide us, that all of us who are in many churches and many communions may be one Church, one Communion and one in him. As he himself earnestly prayed for us in his hour of death, saying, "I pray also for those who through your Word will believe in me, that they may be one as you, Father, are in union with me and I with you, and that they may be one in us," so also we pray. Amen.

Philipp Melanchthon (1497–1560)
German scholar and reformer

O God, in whose one Gospel all are made one, let not your saving work fail in the broken order of Christendom because we have failed to understand your message. Prosper the labors of all Churches bearing the name of Christ and striving to further righteousness and faith in him. Help us to place the truth above our conception of it, and joyfully to recognize the presence of the Holy Spirit wherever he may choose to dwell in human beings; through Jesus Christ our Lord.

Charles Henry Brent (1862–1929)
Episcopal bishop of the Philippines
and Faith and Order leader

O Lord Jesus Christ, you prayed for your disciples that they might be one, even as you are one with the Father: draw us to yourself that in common love and obedience to you we may be united to one another, in the fellowship of the one Spirit, that the world may believe that you are Lord, to the glory of God the Father. Amen.

William Temple (1881–1944)
Archbishop of Canterbury and president of
the Workers' Educational Association

O God, who made of one blood all nations to dwell on the face of the whole earth and who sent your blessed Son to preach peace to those who are far off and to those that are near; grant that all everywhere may seek after you and find you. Bring the nations into your fold, pour out your Spirit upon all flesh, and hasten your kingdom; through the same, your Son, Jesus Christ our Lord.

George E. L. Cotton (1813–1866)
Anglican bishop of Calcutta

O God, you are the light of the world, the desire of all nations, and the shepherd of our souls: let your light shine in the darkness, that all the ends of the earth may see the salvation of our God. By the lifting up of your Cross gather the peoples to your obedience; let your sheep hear your voice, and be brought home to your fold; so that there may be one flock, one shepherd, one holy kingdom of righteousness and peace, one God and Father of all, above all, and in all, and through all.

W. E. Orchard (1877–1955)
Presbyterian minister who became a
Catholic priest and liturgist

Great Shepherd of souls, bring home into your fold all who have gone astray. Preserve your Church from all heresy or schism, from all that persecute or oppose the truth; and give to your ministers wisdom and holiness and the powerful aid of your blessed Spirit.

John Wesley (1703–1791)
Anglican priest and founder of the
Methodist Church

O God, we beg you, make us honest money-changers; that in rendering your eternal Gospel in coin of the present day, we may give full value for what we have received; through Jesus Christ our Lord.

Sherman E. Johnson (b. 1908)
Dean of the Church Divinity School of the
Pacific, Berkeley, California

Lord Jesus Christ, you stretched out your arms of love on the hard wood of the Cross, that all might come within the reach of your saving embrace: so clothe us in your Spirit, that reaching forth our hands in loving labor for others, we may bring those who do not know you to both knowledge and love of you; for the honor of your Holy Name.

Charles Henry Brent

2. For the City and the Nation

O God, grant us a vision of this city, fair as it might be: a city of justice, where none shall prey upon the other; a city of plenty, where vice and poverty shall cease to fester; a city of brotherhood, where success is founded on service, and honor is given to nobleness alone; a city of peace, where order shall not rest on force, but on the love of all for each and all.

Walter Rauschenbusch (1861–1918)
American Baptist minister and exponent of
the Social Gospel

Lord, give us faith that right makes might.

Grant, O merciful God, that with malice towards none, with charity for all, with firmness in the right as you give us to see the right, we may strive to finish the work we are in; to bind up the nation's wounds, . . . to do all which may achieve and cherish a just and lasting peace among ourselves and with all nations; through Jesus Christ our Lord.

Abraham Lincoln (1809–1865)
Sixteenth president of the United States

Most omnipotent, maker and guide of all, who alone searches and fathoms our hearts and truly discerns that no malice of revenge nor desire of bloodshed, nor greed of gain, has bred our resolution: prosper the work we humbly beseech you, guide the journey, speed the victory, and make the return the advancement of your glory and the safety of this realm.

Queen Elizabeth I of England (1533–1603),
at the departure of the Fleet in 1596

O God, the God of all righteousness, mercy, and love, give us all grace and strength to conceive and execute whatever may be for your honor and the welfare of the nation, that we may become at last, through the merits and intercession of our common Redeemer, a great and a happy, because a wise and understanding people, to your honor and glory.

Lord Salisbury (1830–1903)
English prime minister

O God our Father, make us worthy of your trust which you have placed in us. May we have bravery and devotion which befit these times. As a nation may we have the warm courage of unity and the clear consciousness of seeking tried and precious moral values. As citizens may we have the clean satisfaction that comes from the stern performance of our duty. May we have faith in the future of democracy and may we build for a world of lasting brotherhood and peace. Amen.

Franklin Delano Roosevelt (1882–1945)
Thirty-second president of the United States

Almighty God, we make our earnest prayer that you will keep the United States in your holy protection; that you will incline the hearts of the citizens to cultivate a spirit of subordination and obedience to government, and entertain a brotherly affection and love for one another and for their fellow-citizens of the United States at large. And, finally, that you will most graciously be pleased to dispose us all to do justice, to love mercy, and to demean ourselves with that charity, humility, and pacific temper of mind which were the characteristics of the Divine Author of our blessed religion and without which we can never be a happy nation. Grant our supplication, we beseech you, through Jesus Christ our Lord. Amen.

George Washington (1732–1799)
First president of the United States

Almighty God, supreme Governor of all, incline your ear, we beg you, to the prayer of nations, and so overrule the imperfect counsel of human beings, and set straight the things they cannot govern, that we may walk in paths of obedience to places of vision, and to thoughts that purge and make us wise; through Jesus Christ our Lord.

Woodrow Wilson (1856–1924)
Twenty-eighth president of the United States

O Lord, we beg you to govern the minds of all who are called at this time to choose faithful persons into the great counsel of the nation; that they may exercise their choice as in your sight, for the welfare of all our people; through Jesus Christ our Lord.

Charles Gore (1853–1932)
Bishop of Worcester, Birmingham, and Oxford

O heavenly Father, at whose hand the weak shall take no wrong nor the mighty escape just judgment; pour your grace upon your servants our judges and magistrates, that by their true, fruitful and diligent execution of justice to all equally, you may be glorified, the commonwealth daily promoted, and we all live in peace and quietness, godliness and virtue; through Jesus Christ our Lord.

Thomas Cranmer (1489–1556)
Archbishop of Canterbury and editor in
chief of the Book of Common Prayer

Lord Jesus,
    You were in prison, found guilty when you were innocent;
    You were executed as traitor when in fact you were Savior.
To you who died to set all free we pray for:
    All makers of the laws of the land, that they do so with reason and compassion.
    All interpreters of the law—judges, lawyers—that they be fair, honest and impartial.
    All administrators of the law—prison guards and superintendents—that they be merciful in their firmness.
    All prisoners—that they may know that you are in prison with them, in their homes with their loved ones, and that in you is their hope. Though bound, may they be perfectly free in you and in your service.

John B. Coburn (b. 1914)
Bishop of Massachusetts

O Lord God of time and eternity,
   who makes us creatures of time
that, when time is over,
   we may attain your blessed eternity;
With time, your gift,
   give us also wisdom to redeem the time
      lest our day of grace be lost;
         for our Lord Jesus' sake.

> *Christina Rossetti (1830–1894)*
> *English poet*

Almighty God, from whom all thoughts of truth and peace proceed; kindle, we pray you, in the hearts of all the true love of peace; and guide with your pure and peaceable wisdom those who take counsel for the nations of the earth; that in tranquility your kingdom may go forward, till the earth be filled with the knowledge of your love: through Jesus Christ our Lord. Amen.

> *Francis Paget (1851–1911)*
> *Bishop of Oxford*

3. For Friends, Lovers, Families, and Mentors

For our absent loved ones we implore your loving-kindness. Keep them in life, keep them in glowing honor; and for us, grant that we remain worthy of their love. For Christ's sake, let not our beloved blush for us, nor we for them. Grant us but that, and grant us courage to endure lesser ills unshaken, and to accept death, loss, and disappointment as it were straws upon the tide of life.

> *Robert Louis Stevenson (1850–1894)*
> *Scottish essayist, novelist, and poet*

We invoke your gentlest blessings, our Father, on all true lovers. We praise you for the great longing that draws the soul of man and maid together and bids them leave all the dear bonds of the past to cleave to one another. We thank you for the revealing power of love which divines in the one beloved the mystic beauty and glory of humanity. We thank you for the transfiguring power of love which ripens and ennobles our nature, calling forth the hidden stores of tenderness and strength, and overcoming the selfishness of youth by the passion of self-surrender.

Walter Rauschenbusch (1861–1918)
American Baptist minister and exponent of
the Social Gospel

Deliver us, good Lord, from the excessive demands of business and social life that limit family relationship; from the insensitivity and harshness of judgment that prevent understanding; from domineering ways and selfish imposition of our will; from softness and indulgence mistaken for love. Bless us with wise and understanding hearts that we may demand neither too much nor too little, and grant us such a measure of love that we may nurture our children to that fullness of manhood and womanhood, which you purposed for them, through Jesus Christ our Lord.

Charles S. Martin (b. 1906)
Headmaster of St. Alban's School,
Washington, D.C.

Almighty God and heavenly Father, whose Son Jesus Christ was subject to Mary and Joseph at Nazareth, and shared there the life of an earthly home; send down your blessing, we beg you, upon all Christian families. Grant to parents the spirit of understanding and wisdom; give to the children a spirit of obedience and true reverence; and so bind each to each with the bond of mutual love, that to all its members of whatsoever age, every Christian family may be an image of the Holy Family of Nazareth.

Edward C. Ratcliffe (1896–1967)
Liturgist, regius professor of Divinity,
Cambridge University

Heavenly Father, from whom all fatherhood in heaven and earth is named, bless, we beg you, all children, and give to their parents and to all in whose charge they may be, your Spirit of wisdom and love; so that the home in which they grow up may be to them an image of your kingdom, and the care of their parents a likeness of your love; through Jesus Christ our Lord.

Leslie Hunter (b. 1890)
Bishop of Sheffield

Give, I pray you, to all children grace reverently to love their parents, and lovingly to obey them. Teach us all that filial duty never ends or lessens; and bless all parents in their children, and all children in their parents.

Christina Rossetti (1830–1894)
English poet

Lord Jesus, merciful and patient, grant us grace, I beg you, ever to teach in the teachable spirit; learning along with those we teach, and learning from them whenever you please. Word of God, speak to us, speak by us what you will. Wisdom of God, instruct us . . . that we and they may all be taught of God.

Christina Rossetti

O God, who taught the hearts of your faithful people by sending them the light of your Holy Spirit; bless and direct those to whom the office of teacher is committed; give them wisdom to understand the varied scene of life and to see your purpose as it unfolds; keep their spirits young and fresh that they may understand the aspirations and needs of learners; and so bind teacher and pupil together in a fellowship of discovery that your presence may be seen in their midst; through Jesus Christ our Lord.

Sherman E. Johnson (b. 1908)
Dean of the Church Divinity School
of the Pacific, Berkeley, California

Grant, O Lord, to all teachers and students, to know what is worth knowing, to love what is worth loving, to praise what pleases you most, and to dislike whatsoever is evil in your sight. Grant us with true judgment to distinguish things that differ, and above all to search out and do what is well-pleasing to you, through Jesus Christ our Lord.

Thomas à Kempis (1379–1471)
Dutch mystic, ecclesiastic, and writer

4. For Workers and Immigrants

O Lord, I remember before you all the workers of the world:
Workers with hand or brain:
Workers in cities or in the fields:
Those who go forth to toil and those who keep house:
Employers and employees:
Those who command and those who obey:
Those whose work is dangerous:
Those whose work is monotonous or mean:
Those who can find no work to do:
Those whose work is the service of the poor
Or the healing of the sick
Or the proclamation of the Gospel of Christ
At home or in foreign places.

John Baillie (1886–1960)
Professor of Divinity, Edinburgh University

O God, you have bound us together in this bundle of life; give us grace to understand how our lives depend upon the courage, the industry, the honesty, and the integrity of our fellows; that we may be mindful of their needs, grateful for their faithfulness and faithful in our responsibilities to them; through Jesus Christ our Lord.

Reinhold Niebuhr (1892–1971)
Professor of Applied Christian Ethics,
Union Theological Seminary, New York

O God, we beseech you, give us that world in which it shall be accounted shame and meanness for employers to tyrannize and for workmen to shirk, in which human consciences will not permit people in any land to starve or the few to enjoy leisure at the expense of the many, and in which all children shall have the right to the same opportunities for education. If the way to this order shall lie through pain and sorrow and struggle, give us the patience and the fortitude to bear it in view of the brighter day to come. And in your good time transform that better order into the kingdom of your love; through Jesus Christ our Lord.

Sherman E. Johnson (b. 1908)
Dean of the Church Divinity School of the
Pacific, Berkeley, California

O God, the Father of us all, we praise you for having bound humanity in a great unity of life so that each must lean on the strength of all, and depend for his comfort and safety on the help and labor of his brothers and sisters.

We invoke your blessing on all the men and women who have toiled to build and warm our homes, to fashion our clothing, and to wrest from sea and land the food that nourishes us and our children.

We pray you that they may have health and joy, and hope and love, even as we desire for our loved ones.

Grant us wisdom to deal justly with every man and woman whom we face in the business of life.

May we not unknowingly inflict suffering through selfish indifference or the willful ignorance of a callous heart. . . .

May the time come when we need wear and use nothing that is

wet in your sight with human tears, or cheapened by wearing down the lives of the weak.

Speak to our souls and bid us strive for the coming of your kingdom of justice when your merciful and saving will shall be done on earth.

Walter Rauschenbusch (1861–1918)
American Baptist minister and
exponent of the Social Gospel

O God, great champion of the outcast and the weak, we remember before you the people of other nations who are coming to our land seeking bread, a home, and a future. May we look with your compassion upon those who have been drained and stunted by the poverty and oppression of centuries, and whose minds have been warped by superstition or seared by the dumb agony of revolt. We bless you for all that America has meant to the alien folk that have crossed the sea in the past, and for all the patient strength and God-fearing courage with which they have enriched our nation. We rejoice in the millions whose life has expanded in the wealth and liberty of our country, and whose children have grown to fairer stature and larger thoughts; for we, too, are the children of immigrants who came with anxious hearts and halting feet on the westward path of hope.

Walter Rauschenbusch

5. For Those in Difficulty

O Father, you who in your grace give us the companions of our hearts and unite them to us with bonds of undying love, comfort your sorrowing children. May they think of their beloved as still with you. Let the memory of saintly lives strengthen their faith and hope and love. Grant them grace to return with courage to their home and work, and to discharge their duties with fidelity to you and loyalty to those whose trust and affection they share. Enable them to serve their generation with patience and devotion as fellow-citizens with the saints in light, and unite them with those who before have entered into your eternal city, through Jesus Christ, the Way, the Truth, and the Life.

Henry Sloane Coffin (1877–1954)
Minister of Madison Avenue Presbyterian
Church and president of Union
Theological Seminary, New York

O loving Father, we pray for all who are handicapped in the race of life. . . . We pray for those worn with sickness and those who are wasted with misery, for the dying and all unhappy children. May they learn the mystery of the road of suffering which Christ has trodden and the saints have followed, and bring you this gift that angels cannot bring, a heart that trusts you even in the dark; and this we ask in the name of him who himself took our infirmities upon him, even the same Jesus Christ, our Savior.

A. S. T. Fisher (1906–1988)
Fellows' chaplain, Magdalen College, Oxford

Almighty God, look upon those who are in need but cannot work, or who lack employment and search for it in vain: on those who struggle to meet exacting claims with inadequate resources: on all who move in insecurity, attended by worry or despair. Stand by them, O God, in their deprivations, their dilemmas, and guide them as they try to solve their problems; let them come to open doors of opportunity or refuge; and so quicken and extend the world's concern for all those people that everyone may be ensured a livelihood and safety from the bitterness of want; through Jesus Christ our Lord.

Miles Lowell Yates (1890–1956)
American Anglican clergyman

Comfort, we beg you, most gracious God, this your servant, cast down and faint of heart amidst the sorrows and difficulties of the world; and grant that, by the power of your Holy Spirit, he [she] may be enabled to go upon his [her] way rejoicing, and give you continual thanks for your sustaining providence; through Jesus Christ our Lord.

Richard Meux Benson (1824–1915)
Founder of the Anglican Society of Mission
Priests of St. John the Evangelist

We bring before you, O Lord, the troubles and perils of people and nations, the sighing of prisoners and captives, the sorrows of the bereaved, the necessities of strangers, the helplessness of the weak, the despondency of the weary, the failing powers of the aged. O Lord, draw near to each; for the sake of Jesus Christ our Lord. Amen.

St. Anselm (1033–1109)
Philosopher, archbishop of Canterbury

6. For Animals

O God, you created all living things on the face of the earth and gave us dominion over them: grant that we may be faithful to this trust in the way we treat animals, both wild and tame. Teach us to admire their beauty and to delight in their cunning; to respect their strength and to wonder at their intelligence. Grant that our use of them may be both merciful and wise. So may we lend our voice to the praise of your goodness which endures for ever.

Charles Philip Price (b. 1920)
Preacher to Harvard University

O God, my Master, should I gain the grace
To see you face to face, when life is ended,
Grant that a little dog, who once pretended
That I was God, may see me face to face.

Francis Jammes (1868–1938)
French poet and novelist
(prayer translated by B. C. Boulter)

PART 5

PRAYERS MARKING TIMES

1. For Morning and Evening

I rise and pledge myself to God
to do no deed at all of dark.
This day shall be his sacrifice
and I, unmoved, my passions' lord.
I blush to be so old and foul
and yet to stand before his table.
You know what I would do, O Christ;
O then, to do it make me able.

Gregory of Nazianzus (c.330–c.389)
Theologian of the Eastern Orthodox Church
and Cappadocian Father

Christ, whose glory fills the skies,
    Christ, the true and only light,
Sun of righteousness, arise,
    Triumph o'er the shades of night;
Dayspring from on high, be near;
Daystar, in my heart appear!

Visit, then, this soul of mine,
    Pierce the gloom of sin and grief;
Fill me, Radiancy divine
    Scatter all my unbelief;
More and more Thyself display,
Shining to the perfect day!

Charles Wesley (1707–1788)
Methodist preacher and hymnwriter

Father in heaven! When the thought of you wakes in our hearts,
let it not awaken like a frightened bird that flies about in dismay,
but like a child waking from its sleep with a heavenly smile.

Søren Kierkegaard (1813–1855)
Danish philosopher and theologian

We resign into your hands our sleeping bodies, our cold hearths
and open doors. Give us to awaken with smiles; give us to labor
smiling. As the sun returns in the east, so let our patience be
renewed with dawn; as the sun lightens the world, so let our
loving-kindness make bright this house of our habitation.

Robert Louis Stevenson (1850–1894)
Scottish essayist, novelist, and poet

O Lord, support us all the day long, until the shadows lengthen and the evening comes, and the busy world is hushed, and the fever of life is over, and our work is done. Then in your mercy grant us a safe lodging, and a holy rest, and peace at the last.

John Henry Newman (1801–1890)
Cardinal, theologian, and man of letters

Most great and mighty God, you are the sovereign Lord of heaven and earth, the Creator, the Preserver and Governor of all things. You dwell in that light which no mortal eye can approach, and yet you do not disdain to behold our darkened souls. Look down, we beg you, on us your unworthy creatures. We humbly thank you for your daily care of us. We beg your pardon for whatsoever you have seen amiss in us this day, in our thoughts, words, or actions. Strengthen us in every good purpose and resolution. Reform whatsoever you see amiss in the temper and disposition of our minds or in any of the habits of our lives; that we may love you more and serve you better, and do your will with greater care and diligence than we have yet done.

In the name of Jesus Christ our only Lord and Savior.

Warren Hastings (1732–1818)
English colonial administrator

O most merciful Father, take us, we beg you, into your gracious protection this night. Preserve us, if it be your good will, in health and safety; and grant us that rest which may refresh our bodies and dispose us to serve you cheerfully both in body and mind the ensuing day.

We heartily desire the good of all people, and pray to you for the relief and comfort of all that are in trouble, for all our friends and relations, especially those who are most dear to us, begging you to hear and to accept us and them, and all that call upon you in the name of Jesus Christ, our only Lord and Savior.

Warren Hastings

O Holy Jesus, who had no place to lay your head, watch with me in the night hours, I pray you; calm my fears and relieve my anxieties with your blessed gift of sleep; give me your peace and grant that I may wake up refreshed in your service; who with the Father and the Holy Spirit rules all things.

Robert N. Rodenmayer (1909–1979)
American Episcopal priest and anthologist

2. For the Blessings of Marriage

The Lord sanctify and bless you,
the Lord pour the riches of his grace upon you,
that you may please him
and live together in holy love
to your lives' end.
So be it.

John Knox (1513–1572)
Scottish reformer

O God, out of all the world you let us find one another and learn together the meaning of love. Let us never fail to hold love precious. Let the flame of it never waver or grow dim, but burn in our hearts as an unwavering devotion and shine through our eyes in gentleness and understanding on which no shadow falls. . . . Teach us to remember the little courtesies, to be swift to speak the grateful and happy word, to believe rejoicingly in each other's best, and to face all life bravely because we face it with united heart. . . . Through Jesus Christ our Lord. Amen.

Walter Russell Bowie (1882–1969)
Rector of Grace Episcopal Church,
New York City

That I may come near to her,
draw me nearer to you than to her;
that I may know her,
make me to know you more than her;
that I may love her
with the love of a perfectly whole heart,
cause me to love you more than her and most of all.

Temple Gairdner (1873–1928)
Anglican missionary to Cairo and translator
of numerous hymns, poems, and plays

3. For the Gift of Children

Bless my children with healthful bodies, with good understandings, with the graces and gifts of your Spirit, with sweet
dispositions and holy habits, and sanctify them throughout in
their bodies and souls and spirits, and keep them unblamable to
the coming of the Lord Jesus.

Jeremy Taylor (1613–1667)
English writer and Anglican bishop

Almighty God and heavenly Father, we thank you for the children
whom you have given to us; give us also grace to train them in
your faith, fear and love, that as they advance in years they may
grow in grace, and be found hereafter in the number of your elect
children; through Jesus Christ our Lord.

John Cosin (1594–1672)
Bishop of Durham and one of the revisers of
the Book of Common Prayer

4. For the Dying and the Dead

O God, whose most dear Son took little children into his arms and blessed them; give us grace, we beg you, to entrust the soul of this child to your never-failing care and love, and bring us all to your heavenly kingdom; through the same, your Son, Jesus Christ our Lord.

John Dowden (1840–1910)
Bishop of Edinburgh and writer

May we become as this little child who now follows the child Jesus, that Lamb of God in a white robe, wherever he goes; even so, Lord Jesus. You gave him [her] to us, you have taken him [her] from us. Blessed be the name of the Lord. Amen.

John Evelyn (1620–1706)
English diarist

Grant, almighty God, that, since the dullness and harshness of our flesh is so great that it is needful for us in various ways to be afflicted, we may patiently bear your chastisement, and under a deep feeling of sorrow flee to your mercy displayed to us in Christ; and that, not depending upon the earthly blessings of this perishable life, but relying only upon your Word, we may go forward in the course of our calling; until at length we are gathered to that blessed rest which is laid up for us in heaven; through Jesus Christ our Lord.

John Calvin (1509–1564)
French theologian and reformer in Geneva

Almighty God, my Creator and Preserver, who has permitted me to begin another year, look with mercy upon my wretchedness and frailty. Rectify my thoughts, relieve my perplexities, strengthen my purposes, and reform my doings. Let increase of years bring increase of faith, hope and charity. Grant me diligence in whatever work your providence shall appoint me. Take not from me your Holy Spirit, but let me pass the remainder of the days which you shall allow me, in your fear and to your glory; and when it shall be your good pleasure to call me hence, grant me, O Lord, forgiveness of my sins, and receive me to everlasting happiness, for the sake of Jesus Christ, our Lord. Amen.

Samuel Johnson (1709–1784)
English writer and lexicographer

Almighty and most merciful Father, I am now, as to human eyes it seems, about to commemorate, for the last time, the death of your Son Jesus Christ our Savior and Redeemer. Grant, O Lord, that my whole hope and confidence may be in his merits and his mercy; enforce and accept my imperfect repentance; make this commemoration confirm my faith, establish my hope and enlarge my charity, and make the death of your Son Jesus Christ effectual to my redemption. Have mercy upon me and pardon the multitude of my offenses. Bless my friends, have mercy upon all. Support me, by the grace of your Holy Spirit, in the days of weakness and at the hour of death; and receive me, at my death, to everlasting happiness, for the sake of Jesus Christ. Amen.

Samuel Johnson

Lord, grant that while I live I may do what service I may do in this frail body, and be in continual expectation of my change, and let me never forget your great love to my soul so lately expressed, when I could lie down and bequeath my soul to you, and death seemed no terrible thing. O let me ever see you who are invisible, and I shall not be unwilling to come, though by so rough a messenger. Amen.

Anne Bradstreet (1612–1672)
New England poet and Puritan

Eternal Father, you alone can control the days that are gone and the deeds that are done; remove from my burdened memory the weight of past years, that being set free both from the glamor of complacency and from the palsy of remorse, I may reach forth unto those things which are before, and press towards the mark for the prize of the high calling of God in Christ Jesus.

Charles Henry Brent (1862–1929)
Episcopal bishop of the Philippines and
Faith and Order leader

We commit to your care, O Lord, those who are old and full of years, and can no longer bear the burden and heat of the day. Grant them to have so trusted and learned of you in years which are gone, that in the loss of their daily work and the world they have long known, they shall not have lost you. Give them light at evening time, and the assurance that, by serene example, they may also serve who only stand and wait; through Jesus Christ our Lord.

Willard Sperry (1882–1954)
Dean of Harvard Divinity School and
Congregational clergyman

O Jesus, be mindful of your promise; think of us, your servants; and when we shall depart hence, speak to our soul these loving words: "Today you shall be with me in joy." O Lord Jesus Christ, remember us your servants who trust in you, when our tongues cannot speak, when the sight of our eyes fails, and when our ears are stopped. . . . Let our soul always rejoice in you and be joyful about your salvation, which you through your death have purchased for us.

Miles Coverdale (c.1488–1569)
English reformer and translator of
  the Bible

Lord, though I am a miserable and wretched creature, I am in Covenant with you through grace. And I may, I will, come to you, for your people. You have made me, though very unworthy, a mean instrument to do them some good, and you service; and many of them have set too high a value upon me, though others wish and would be glad of my death; Lord, however you dispose of me, continue and go on to do good for them. Give them consistency of judgment, one heart, and mutual love; and go on to deliver them, and with the work of reformation; and make the name of Christ glorious in the world. Teach those who look too much on your instruments, to depend more on yourself. Pardon such as desire to trample on the dust of a poor worm, for they are your people too. And pardon the folly of this short prayer—even for Jesus Christ's sake. And give us a good night, if it be your pleasure.

Oliver Cromwell (1599–1658)
Puritan Lord Protector of England

When the signs of age begin to mark my body (and still more when they touch my mind); when the ill that is to diminish me or carry me off strikes from without or is born within me; when the painful moment comes in which I suddenly awaken to the fact that I am ill or growing old; and above all at that last moment when I feel I am losing hold of myself and am absolutely passive within the hands of the great unknown forces that have formed me; in all those dark moments, O God, grant that I may understand that it is you (provided only my faith is strong enough) who are painfully parting the fibers of my being in order to penetrate to the very marrow of my substance and bear me away within yourself.

Teilhard de Chardin (1881–1955)
French Jesuit, paleontologist, and
philosopher

Into your hands, O merciful Savior, we commend the soul of your servant now departed from the body. Acknowledge, we humbly beg you, a sheep of your own fold, a lamb of your own flock, a sinner of your own redeeming. Receive him [her] into the arms of your mercy, into the blessed rest of everlasting peace and into the glorious company of the saints in light.

John Cosin (1594–1672)
Bishop of Durham and one of the revisers of
the Book of Common Prayer

PART 6

PRAYERS FOR THE CHRISTIAN YEAR

1. Advent

O God, who looked on us when we had fallen down into death, and resolved to redeem us by the Advent of your only begotten Son; grant, we beg you, that those who confess his glorious Incarnation may also be admitted to the fellowship of their Redeemer, through the same Jesus Christ our Lord.

St. Ambrose (339–397)
Bishop of Milan

2. Christmas Eve

Send, O God, into the darkness of this troubled world, the light of your Son: let the star of your hope touch the minds of all people with the bright beams of mercy and truth; and so direct our steps that we may always walk in the way revealed to us, as the shepherds of Bethlehem walked with joy to the manger where he dwelt who now and ever reigns in our hearts, Jesus Christ our Lord.

John Wallace Suter (1890–1977)
Dean of Washington Cathedral

3. Christmas Day

I would I were some bird or star,
Fluttering in woods or lifted far
    Above this inn,
    And road of sin!
Then either star or bird should be
Shining or singing still to Thee.

I would I had in my best part
Fit rooms for Thee! Or that my heart
    Were so clean as
    Thy manger was!
But I am all filth, and obscene;
Yet, if thou wilt, Thou canst make clean.

Sweet Jesus! will then; let no more
This leper haunt and soil thy door!
    Cure him, ease him,
    O release him!
And let once more, by mystic birth,
The Lord of life be born on earth.

Henry Vaughan (c.1621–1695)
Welsh metaphysical poet

As we celebrate today the octave of Christ's birth, we revere the marvels you wrought, Lord, when he was born: for she that gave him birth was a virgin mother, and he that was born of her was a child-God.

No wonder was it that the heavens gave tongue, the angels rejoiced, the Magi underwent a transformation, kings were seized with anxiety and tiny children were crowned with the glory of martyrdom. He was our Food, yet his mother fed him; he was the Bread that came from heaven, yet he was laid in the manger like fodder, for the animals to eat devoutly.

There did the ox recognize its owner and the ass its Master's crib: there did the people of the circumcision acknowledge him, there did the Gentiles acclaim him. This figure too did our Lord fulfill to the utmost, when of his kindness he was taken in Simeon's arms in the Temple.

The Gelasian Sacramentary

4. For the New Year

Eternal God, you make all things new, and abide for ever the same: grant us to begin this year in your faith, and to continue it in your favor; that, being guided in all our doings, and guarded all our days, we may spend our lives in your service, and finally, by your grace, attain the glory of everlasting life; through Jesus Christ our Lord.

W. E. Orchard (1877–1955)
Presbyterian minister who became a
Catholic priest and liturgist

5. Ash Wednesday

Give me grace, O my Father, to be utterly ashamed of my own reluctance. Rouse me from sloth and coldness, and make me desire you with my whole heart. Teach me to love meditation, sacred reading, and prayer. Teach me to love that which must engage my mind for all eternity.

John Henry Newman (1801–1890)
Cardinal, theologian, and man of letters

6. Palm Sunday

All glory, laud and honor, to Thee, Redeemer, King!
To whom the lips of children made sweet hosannas ring.
Thou art the King of Israel, Thou, David's royal Son,
Who in the Lord's name comest, the King and blessed One.

St. Theodulf of Orléans (c.750–c.821)
Poet and leading theologian of the
Frankish Empire

Almighty God, we who know the bondage of fear celebrate today the invincible joy of Jesus Christ our Lord: the sight of him, humble but unswerving, entering the city of darkest hate, holding the gift of gladness from little children against the priest's complaint, unafraid of the fate of death, as though all this was his day's work, redeems us from our own cowardice and confusion. Grant us too the triumph of the soul's joy against the empty pleasure of the world's applause, through Jesus Christ. Amen.

Samuel H. Miller (1900–1968)
Dean of Harvard Divinity School
and Baptist minister

As on this day we keep the special memory of our Redeemer's entry into the city, so grant, O Lord, that now and ever, he may triumph in our hearts. Let the King of grace and glory enter in, and let us lay ourselves and all we are in full and joyful homage before him; through the same Jesus Christ our Lord. Amen.

H. C. G. Moule (1841–1920)
Bishop of Durham

O God, whose dearly beloved Son was greeted by the crowd on Olivet with hallelujahs, but who in that same week was mocked as he went lonely to the Cross, forbid that our welcome to him should be in words alone. Help us, we beg you, to keep the road open for him into our hearts; and let him find there not another crucifixion, but love and loyalty in which his kingdom may be established evermore. Amen.

Walter Russell Bowie (1882–1969)
Rector of Grace Episcopal Church,
New York City

7. Holy Week

Grant, O Lord, that in your wounds I may find my safety, in your stripes my cure, in your pain my peace, in your Cross my victory, in your Resurrection my triumph, and a crown of righteousness in the glories of your eternal kingdom.

Jeremy Taylor (1613–1667)
English writer and Anglican bishop

Lord, you go forth alone to your sacrifice: you offer yourself to death, which you have come to destroy. What can we miserable sinners plead, who know that for the deeds that we have done, you atone? Ours is the guilt, Lord: why then must you suffer torture for our sins? Make our hearts so to share in your Passion, that our fellow-suffering may invite your mercy. This is that night of tears and the three days' eventide of sadness, until the daybreak with the risen Christ and with joy to those that mourn. May we so suffer with thee, Lord, that we may be partners of your glory, and our three days' mourning shall pass away and become your Easter joy.

Peter Abelard (c.1079–1144)
French philosopher and theologian

8. *Good Friday*

Savior, who in human flesh conquered tears by crying, pain by suffering, death by dying, we, your servants, gather before the Cross to commemorate your Passion and to contemplate anew the wonder of your compassionate love. As we listen to your gracious words, uttered with dying lips, illumine our souls that we may know the truth, melt our hearts that we may hate our sins, nerve our wills that we may do your bidding; to the glory of your name and our own eternal gain.

Charles Henry Brent (1862–1929)
Episcopal bishop of the Philippines and
Faith and Order leader

Forgive us that with the Cross as starting point we have made of Christian faith a bland and easy-going way of life.

Forgive us that our preference runs to Bethlehem and Joseph's garden, to poinsettias and lilies, and away from Golgotha, with its rusty nails and twisted thorns.

Forgive us that we are more willing to be instructed or reformed than we are to be redeemed.

Open us, each one, to ever new and deeper meanings in our Savior's Passion.

Ernest T. Campbell (b. 1915)
Minister of Riverside Church, New York City

9. Easter

The day of Resurrection! Earth, tell it out abroad,
The Passover of gladness, the Passover of God.
From death to life eternal, from this world to the sky,
Our Christ has brought us over, with hymns of victory.

> *St. John of Damascus (c.675–749)*
> *Orthodox theologian*

O Christ, the brightness of God's glory and express image of his person, whom death could not conquer, nor the tomb imprison; as you have shared our mortal frailty in the flesh, help us to share your immortal triumph in the spirit. Let no shadow of the grave affright us and no fear of darkness turn our hearts from you. Reveal yourself to us as the first and the last, the Living One, our immortal Savior and Lord. Amen.

> *Henry Van Dyke (1852–1933)*
> *Minister of the Brick Presbyterian Church,*
> *New York City; U.S. ambassador to the*
> *Netherlands and Luxembourg; and author*

O God, you manifested yourself in the breaking of bread to your disciples at Emmaus, grant us ever through the same blessed Sacrament of your Presence to know you, and to love you more and more with all our hearts. Abide with us, abide in us, that we may ever abide in you; dwell in us that we may ever dwell in you, O good Jesus, God of our salvation.

> *Edward Bouverie Pusey (1800–1882)*
> *Canon of Christ Church and regius*
> *professor of Hebrew, Oxford University*

O God, you have glorified our victorious Savior with a visible, triumphant resurrection from the dead, and ascension into heaven, where he sits at your right hand; grant, we beg you, that his triumphs and glories may ever shine in our eyes, to make us more clearly see through his sufferings, and more courageously endure our own; being assured by his example, that if we endeavor to live and die like him, for the advancement of your love in ourselves and others, you will raise our dead bodies again, and conforming them to his glorious body, call us above the clouds, and give us possession of your everlasting kingdom.

John Wesley (1703–1791)
Anglican priest and founder of the
Methodist Church

10. Pentecost

Be pleased to visit your Church with the Holy Spirit. Renew the day of Pentecost in our midst, and in the midst of all gatherings of your people, may there come the downfall of the holy fire, the uprising of the heavenly wind. May matters that are now slow and dead become quick and full of life, and may the Lord Jesus Christ be exalted in the midst of his Church which is his fullness—"the fullness of him that filleth all in all." May multitudes be converted; may they come flocking to Christ with holy eagerness to find in him a refuge as the doves fly to their dovecotes.

Charles H. Spurgeon (1834–1892)
English Baptist minister and
biblical expositor

11. Trinity Sunday

Most blessed and glorious Trinity, Three Persons in one God, teach us to worship and adore that absolute Trinity, that perfect Unity. And that we may adore you, that our worship may not be a mockery, make us to know that we are one in Christ, as the Father is one with the Son, and the Son with the Father. Prevent us from looking upon our sectarianism as if it were a destiny. Help us to regard it as a rebellion against you.

Help us to see all distinctions more clearly in the light of your everlasting love. Help us to recognize the truth of every effort to express something of that which passes knowledge. Help us to feel and confess the feebleness of our own efforts. So may your holy name embrace us more and more. So may all creatures in heaven and earth and under the earth at last glorify you throughout all ages. Amen.

F. D. Maurice (1805–1872)
Anglican theologian, ecumenist, and
Christian Socialist

SOURCES OF THE PRAYERS

Aldrich, Donald B., ed. *The Golden Book of Prayer.* New York: Dodd, Mead, 1942.

Appleton, George, ed. *The Oxford Book of Prayer.* London: Oxford University Press, 1985.

Barclay, William. *A Book of Everyday Prayers.* New York: Harper, 1959.

Binyon, Gilbert Clive, ed. *Prayers for the City of God.* 3rd ed. London: Longmans, Green & Co., 1927.

Boyd, Malcolm. *Are You Running with Me, Jesus?* New York: Holt, Rinehart, 1965.

Coburn, John B. *A Diary of Prayers, Personal and Public.* Philadelphia: Westminster Press, 1975.

Davies, Horton, and Morris Slifer, eds. *Prayers and Other Resources for Public Worship.* Nashville: Abingdon Press, 1976.

Dawson, George. *A Collection of Prayers.* 9th ed. London: Kegan Paul, Trench, Trubner and Co., 1885.

Doughty, W. L., ed. *The Prayers of Susanna Wesley.* Grand Rapids: Zondervan–Clarion Classics, 1984.

Edwards, Charles E., ed. *Devotions and Prayers of John Calvin.* Grand Rapids: Baker Book House, 1954.

Fisher, A. S. T., ed. *An Anthology of Prayers Compiled for Use in School and Home.* London: Longmans, Green & Co., 1934.

Forsyth, P. T. *Intercessory Services.* London: Heywood, 1896.

Fox, Selina F., ed. *A Chain of Prayer across the Ages: Forty Centuries of Prayer, 2000 B.C.–A.D. 1941.* 6th ed. London: John Murray, 1941.

Fritchman, S. H., ed. *Prayers of the Free Spirit.* New York: Woman's Press of the YMCA of the USA, 1945.

Geffen, Roger, ed. *The Handbook of Public Prayer.* New York: Macmillan, 1963.

Gill, F. C., ed. *John Wesley's Prayers.* London: Epworth Press, 1951.

Goodacre, Norman W., ed. *Prayers for Today: Contemporary Material for Worship*. London and Oxford: A. R. Mowbray & Co., 1973.

Hamman, A., ed. *Early Christian Prayers*. Chicago: Henry Regnery Co., 1961.

Hammarskjöld, Dag. *Markings*. London: Faber & Faber, 1964.

Hunt, Cecil, ed. *Uncommon Prayers*. New York: Seabury Press, 1955.

James, Lionel, ed. *Jubilate Deo: A Sequence of Daily Prayers for Schools*. 3rd ed. London: Oxford University Press, 1940.

Macnutt, Frederick B., ed. *The Prayer Manual*. London: A. R. Mowbray & Co., 1951.

Miller, Samuel H. *Prayers for Daily Use*. New York: Harper & Bros., 1957.

Milner-White, E., and G. W. Briggs, eds. *Daily Prayer*. London: Oxford University Press, 1941.

Morrison, James D., ed. *Minister's Service-Book*. New York: Willet Clark & Co., 1937.

Mother Teresa of Calcutta. *Life in the Spirit: Reflections, Meditations, and Prayers*. San Francisco: Harper & Row, 1983.

Noyes, Morgan P., ed. *Prayers for Services: A Manual for Leaders of Worship*. New York: Charles Scribner's Sons, 1934.

Orchard, W. E. *Divine Service*. London: Oxford University Press, 1919.

———. *The Temple*. London: J. M. Dent & Sons, n.d.

Porter, David R., ed. *The Enrichment of Prayer*. New York: Association Press, 1918.

Rauschenbusch, Walter. *Prayers of the Social Awakening*. Boston: Pilgrim Press, 1925.

Rodenmayer, Robert N. *The Pastor's Prayerbook*. New York: Oxford University Press, 1960.

Shepherd, Massey H., Jr., ed. *A Companion of Prayers for Daily Living*. Wilton, Conn.: Morehouse-Barlow Co., 1978.

Spurgeon, C. H. *C. H. Spurgeon's Prayers*. New York: Fleming H. Revell, 1906.

Stevenson, R. L. *Prayers Written at Vailima*. London: Chatto & Windus, 1910.

Suter, John W., ed. *Prayers for a New World*. New York: Charles Scribner's Sons, 1964.

———. *Prayers of the Spirit*. New York: Harper & Bros., 1943.

Thorne, Leo, ed. *Prayers from Riverside*. New York: Pilgrim Press, 1983.

Tileston, Mary W., ed. *Great Souls at Prayer*. London: H. R. Allenson, 1929.

Trueblood, Elton, ed. *Dr. Johnson's Prayers*. New York: Harper & Bros., 1945.

INDEX

Abelard, Peter, 144
Addison, Joseph, 11
Aitken, W. H., 33
Alcuin of York, 18
Alford, Henry, 93
Alfred the Great, 43
Ambrose, St., 56, 92, 139
Andrewes, Lancelot, 67
Anselm, St., 19, 35, 48, 71, 82, 124
Aquinas, St. Thomas, 40, 41, 47
Arnold, Thomas, 63, 102
Astley, Sir Jacob, 29
Augustine of Hippo, St., 17, 34, 68, 70, 75

Bacon, Francis, 68-69
Baillie, John, 120
Barclay, William, 8
Becon, Thomas, 5, 50, 57
Beecher, Henry Ward, 57, 100
Beethoven, Ludwig van, 84, 85
Benedict, St., 62
Benson, Edward White, 24
Benson, Richard Meux, 55, 124
Bernard of Clairvaux, 38
Blake, William, 43
Bonhoeffer, Dietrich, 27-28
Bowie, Walter Russell, 81, 131, 143
Boyd, Malcolm, 103

Bradstreet, Anne, 16, 46, 58, 73, 135
Brent, Charles Henry, 110, 112, 135, 145
Bright, William, 54
Brooks, Phillips, 32, 42
Browne, Sir Thomas, 30
Browning, Robert, 51
Burns, Robert, 10

Calvin, John, 59, 62, 66, 88, 95, 98, 133
Campbell, Ernest T., 32, 145
Campbell, George, 103
Campion, Thomas, 36
Carmichael, Amy, 33
Catherine of Siena, 61
Chalmers, Thomas, 90
Charles I, 36
Chesterton, G. K., 24
Chrysostom, St. John, 26
Coburn, John B., 115
Coffin, Henry Sloane, 60, 123
Coffin, William Sloane, Jr., 93, 107-8
Columba of Iona, St., 96
Cooper, Anthony Ashley, 49
Cosin, John, 132, 137
Cotton, George E. L., 110
Coverdale, Miles, 82, 136
